The World of Serendipity

The World of Serendipity

by

Marcus Bach

PRENTICE-HALL, INC.
Englewood Cliffs, N.J.

The World of Serendipity by Marcus Bach

© 1970 by Marcus Bach

Library of Congress Catalog Card Number: 75-129820

Printed in the United States of America · T

ISBN 0-13-968248-1

Prentice-Hall International, Inc., London
Prentice-Hall of Australia, Pty. Ltd., Sydney
Prentice-Hall of Canada, Ltd., Toronto
Prentice-Hall of India Private Ltd., New Delhi
Prentice-Hall of Japan, Inc., Tokyo

Fondly Dedicated To
Joe Gilbert

CONTENTS

1
THE THING
CALLED CHANCE

*I*f you have ever wondered whether life has any tricks up its sleeve, the answer is definitely, "Yes!" Most everyone agrees to that. But only a few have learned the secret of turning the tricks of life to good advantage or to catching on to the magic of the thing called chance.

I found this secret neatly packaged in a single word: *serendipity*. When I discovered what it meant and how it worked, I was never quite the same again. There is nothing more unique than serendipity, there is nothing more exciting, and, when you come right down to it, there is probably nothing you can use oftener and to greater advantage than the serendipity technique.

But first, some background to our story.

Once upon a time, in the eighteenth century to be exact, there lived an Englishman named Horace Walpole. Though he was Earl of Oxford, a graduate of Eton College and a member of Parliament, he was best known for his passion for writing letters. In fact, if you go into any good-sized library and ask for the correspondence of Horace Walpole, the books containing his letters will probably be brought to you in a shopping cart. There are volumes and volumes of them. Walpole made copies of every letter he wrote and also copies of the answers he received, and this in a day before typewriters or carbon sheets. As an example, to just one of his many correspondents, Sir Horace Mann, an envoy to Florence, Italy, Walpole wrote 848 letters and Mann replied 848 times. That makes 1,696 letters right there.

For most of his life (Walpole lived to be eighty), he kept the postman busy lugging mail away from his home on Strawberry Hill, Twickenham, and lugging back mail from Horace Mann (who lived to be eighty-four).

Important for our purpose is a single letter that Walpole wrote to Mann one cold and foggy winter's day, January 28, 1754. On this occasion, he dipped his quill pen deeper than usual into personal reminiscences and confessed to Sir Horace that an old Persian "fairy tale" had made a profound impression on his life.

The tale, he explained, had to do with "The Three Princes of Serendip" (an ancient name for Ceylon). These three young noblemen, while traveling through the world, rarely found the treasures they were looking for, but continually ran into other treasures equally great or even greater which they were *not* seeking. In looking for one thing they found something else, and it dawned on them that this was one of life's sly and wonderful tricks. When they realized this they got an entirely new slant on life, and every day resulted in a new and thrilling experience.

Even though their goals eluded them, they were more than rewarded with their wayside discoveries, and soon it was as if an unseen power and guidance seemed to know, better than they knew, what was best for them in the long run of search and discovery.

That was the gist of the "fairy tale." When the princes began to "dip" into life with "serenity" (the real meaning of seren-dip-ity) everything that happened was exciting. They had what Walpole called a thrilling approach to life. "That is the way things often happen to me," said Walpole, "when I dip into things. It is as if I had a talisman that came to my aid in the nick of time."

After 1754 the word serendipity lay practically unnoticed for a hundred years. Then scholars stumbled on to it and it began to be talked about and written about and even found its way into some early dictionaries. For example, the dictionary of Sir James A. H. Murray defined the word as, "Making discoveries by accident and sagacity of things not in quest of," or "The faculty of making happy and unexpected discoveries by accident."

I first found the word through one of my own serendipitous experiences several years ago. While doing research in the history of healing. I accidentally ran into the autobiography of Walter B. Cannon in which this noted physician had a chapter titled "Gains from Serendipity." This was exciting reading and in it Cannon cited what he thought was one of the very earliest and best of all serendipity examples. It had to do with the Biblical account of Saul, and when I read Cannon's interpretation of it, my respect for serendipity was full and complete.

Here is how the story went. Saul, the son of Kish, was "a handsome young man. There was none among the people of Israel more handsome than he; from his shoulders upward he was taller than any of the people." Nothing was said about his ambitions or what he was looking for in life, but one day his father, Kish, gave him an assignment. "Take one of the servants with you," Kish told his son, "and go and look for the asses" which were lost.

So Saul and the servant started out. We are not told how long they stayed on the hunt for these elusive animals, but we are told they passed through several countries, into the land of Benjamin and on into the land of Zuph. Tracing this from Mount Ephraim on an old Biblical map, I discovered it was quite a walk, and I imagined that whenever anyone asked Saul what he was looking for, he probably shook his head ruefully and told them.

Then Saul got to thinking that it was really quite a waste of time seeking the asses of Kish, and he suggested to the servant that soon his father would become concerned and begin looking for *him*. Then they both got to thinking. They remembered that a prophet, a seer named Samuel, was supposed to be preaching and prophesying in Zuph at about this time, and they decided to go to him and ask him for help. After all, Samuel had a reputation as being an expert in what we would call the field of ESP.

After considerable difficulty they found the prophet and spoke to him.

Samuel listened with a far-away look in his eye. Then he turned to Saul and said, "As for your asses that were lost three days ago, do not set your mind on them, for they have been found." Then Samuel said to Saul, "Has not the Lord anointed you to be prince over his people Israel?"

I had read this Biblical account many times, but not until I found it in Dr. Cannon's chapter on serendipity did it ever make much of an impression on me. It had always been something of a fairy tale, until Cannon reminded me that "Modest Saul, who went out to seek lost asses, was rewarded with a kingdom."

Then and there I caught on to serendipity. Life, I decided, is so constructed that happenings you never expected to happen are actually things that were supposed to happen. And the most important player in the serendipity drama, I told myself, is *you*.

Now when I find myself involved in assignments as elusive and mundane as the one given to Saul, I catch myself saying, "Wait a minute. You may be on your way to something serendipitous!" Every now and then, in a moment of despair, I run into a Samuel who asks me to come up higher, and who makes me feel I might be slated for bigger things. Always, in my day-by-day experiences, I think of the princes of Serendip who, with "sagacity and insight," found meaning in their seemingly accidental goals.

That is why I said at the beginning: If you have ever wondered whether life has any tricks up its sleeve, the answer is definitely, "Yes!" But only a few have learned the secret of turning the tricks of life to good advantage or to catching on to the magic of the thing called chance.

But this, of course, is only the beginning of our story.

2
EXPECTING
THE UNEXPECTED

*I*n my work with college and
university students I am con-
tinually amazed to see how many young people believe
things that I did not believe when I was their age. For
example, any number are convinced that chance happenings
belong in the regular routine of life. In other words, chance
is not chance, it is a prescribed occurrence in the order of
things. These young people are quite ready to expect and
accept the unexpected.

Such reasoning was far from *my* seventeen-year-old or
even my twenty-year-old mind. I had a habit of saying,
"Why did this happen to *me*?" I walked alone many a time
asking myself, "What did I do to deserve *this*?" Many were

the days when I wondered why the unexpected had come home to roost with me.

Nowadays there is a mature, insightful, mystical approach to life among the youth of student age. Not among all of them, to be sure. Some are still as baffled and befuddled about certain sudden situations as I was when I was their age, but, by and large, they are surprisingly mature and astonishingly philosophic about the thing called chance. Many of them are definitely graduates of the school of serendipity.

Webster calls serendipity "the gift of finding valuable or agreeable things not sought for." It refers to the discovery of goals which you stumble into (or which stumble into you) while you are on a search for an altogether different goal. One of the best descriptions of serendipity was given by a justice of the Supreme Court, Benjamin N. Cardozo, when he said, "Like many of the finest things of life, like happiness and tranquillity and fame, the gain that is most precious is not the thing sought, but one that comes of itself in the search for something else."

I have learned the truth of this through a series of slow but sure experiences and it has had a life-changing effect; but to think that young people have already discovered this is, as I have said, a source of wonder.

Take, for example, the case of Alex Reimer, a college sophomore. He told me of an incident at a summer camp where he went to study under a noted art teacher who had a course titled "Perspective." Alex was planning to major in art and the opportunity of this particular summer was big in his plans. So he went to the camp. When the dormitory rooms were assigned by drawing lots, Alex found himself teamed up with a young man who had come to take a course in music. His name was Ruel Amenson and he was blind.

The camp manager asked Alex if he would be kind enough to help Ruel in an orientation of his surroundings. Alex said he would be happy to do so. And he meant it. *He had already learned to see the unexpected good in the unexpected.* At eighteen he was already versed in the art of serendipity.

And because he was versed in the art, he discovered that in describing the surroundings to his roommate, he himself saw things in greater depth. When (as a case in point) he explained to Ruel that there was a vine with purple flowers outside the window, and when he realized how Ruel "saw" these flowers with sensitive tactile "sight," the flowers and the vine became a new and living reality for Alex.

This went on for days and Alex looked forward as eagerly to his moments with Ruel as he did to his class in "Perspective." He confided to me that he had gone to camp to meet a great art instructor and had found an even greater teacher within himself. He called it an LSD experience without the use of LSD.

LSD, by the way—the unpredictable drug taken by many unpredictable people—was itself the result of serendipity. On a spring day in 1943 a young scientist, Albert Hofmann, working in his Basel, Switzerland, laboratory, broke down the components of a sclerotial body of ergot. By chance he got some of the chemical on his tongue and was astonished to find himself in a fantasy world. Sights were intensified, sounds were magnified, and secret doors were opened to weird, kaleidoscopic surroundings. This was not what he had been looking for. His research had been the exploration of sources which ergot held for controlling hemorrhages and influencing the sympathetic nervous system. What Hofmann found was something quite different.

Days later, when he pursued his reactions further and deliberately ingested a dose of the chemical, he again found himself on a psychedelic trip. He had accidentally discovered lysergic acid diethylamide. When he got on his bicycle and drove home, he steered his way ecstatically and dangerously through city streets. He was "in orbit." People were like planets of varying shapes and sizes. Life was suddenly fluid, time slipped into eternity, space merged with infinity, and Hofmann was spinning his pedals in the activated center of a hallucinatory cosmic world.

The rest is now history. The use, abuse, performance, and perversion of LSD ushered in a new era which is commended by some and condemned by others—but recognized by all. According to some interpreters it opened new "doors of perception" and according to others it unlocked a Pandora's box of dangers and death. The point is that LSD was a case of serendipity, and what man does with his discoveries is up to man.

Think how long Hofmann worked before his serendipity breakthrough! Think of the months and years he pedaled his bike to and from his home before the laboratory yielded up its secret. Think how often people must have said, "What does he hope to find, bent over his microscope, holding his test tubes to the light, and boiling up his brews?"

Interestingly enough, the dried sclerotial bodies of the ergot are themselves a lesson in serendipity. Botanists tell us that in certain fungi, these hardened sclerotial masses of interwoven hyplae (threads of vegetation) lie dormant as if dead, until the coming of a favorable opportunity for growth. The thing called chance may actually be a thing called *life* waiting the fullness of time.

A closer look at serendipity suggests that there are actually techniques involved in some of these remarkable discoveries, and the case of the student, Alex Reimer, and the scientist, Albert Hofmann, illustrate the point. Both were possessed of three qualifications: (1) great expectations, (2) great sublimations, (3) great observations.

I can best illustrate what I mean from my own career. I love to write. I have been writing all my life and no manuscript ever goes on its way to a publisher without a special good-luck blessing. I affirm that the manuscript will be accepted, that the publisher will like it, that the public will welcome it, and that the book will sell. I have absolute, unquestioned faith in my high and holy expectations!

But every once in a while a manuscript comes back.

It is then that I draw on my great sublimations, and this is where my faith in serendipity comes in. I affirm that though I did not reach the initial goal, there will be a wayside goal just as good, or better, waiting for me.

In some twenty-five years of writing, every manuscript of mine that was rejected eventually turned out advantageously for me. Either I improved it, profited from the rejection, placed it elsewhere, adapted it for radio or television, or benefited in some way from its return. I can only conclude that if things work this way with manuscripts, they work this way with life if we are sincerely serendipitous and hold to both great expectations and great sublimations.

Then there is also the matter of great observations.

The Princes of Serendip, from whom the word *serendipity* originated, developed this third quality to an amazingly high degree. They began to see such immense possibilities in the power of observation that some people insisted they were either clairvoyant or spirit-possessed. The story goes that on one occasion they met a man who had lost his camel. When he asked the Princes whether they had perhaps seen the animal, one of the Princes said, "Was your camel blind in the right eye?"

"He was," said the camel driver.

"Did he have a tooth missing?"

"He did."

"Was he lame in the right hind leg?"

"Quite so," said the man.

"And was your camel carrying a load of honey on one side and a load of butter on the other?"

"Correct!" cried the camel driver.

"Well, we saw it some time ago and it must be somewhere behind along the road."

The truth of the matter was that they had not seen the camel at all. When it was not found and they were accused of having stolen it, they explained to the Emperor, who had them arrested, how their uncanny divination had taken place. They explained that they had noticed camel tracks which showed that the right hind hoof made a dragging mark in the road. Obviously it must have been lame. It was blind in the right eye because only the grass on the left side of the trail had been eaten, even though the grass on the right was more lush. Cuds of grass left along the way betrayed the fact that the animal must have had a missing tooth. As for the honey and the butter, they had observed that on one side of the trail a great many flies had been drawn by the scent of honey and on the other side swarms of ants had been attracted by the telltale signs of melted butter.

Greatly impressed, the Emperor asked them where they were going. When they informed him that they were seeking their fortune at some distant goal, he advised them that they had found an even greater fortune by meeting him, and they became the most honored people in the kingdom. Few were the subjects who did not know about the wonderful Princes of Serendip.

Great expectations, great sublimations, great observations.

All figure more importantly than anyone knows in the thing called chance. Which is why Justice Cardozo's saying is especially worth remembering: "Like many of the finest things of life, like happiness and tranquillity and fame, the gain that is most precious is not the thing sought, but one that comes of itself in the search for something else."

3
THE CASE
FOR PROBABILITIES

$\mathcal{S}$erendipity makes me wonder. Do things simply happen or are they brought about? Is it possible that Chance is a nickname for Providence? Or can it be, as Anatole France once observed, "Chance is the pseudonym God uses when He does not want to sign His name?"

However it may be, I am thoroughly convinced that while there are times when I take chances, there are even more times when chances take *me,* a fact that becomes clear when we consider "The Case for Probabilities."

There are three things to learn from probabilities: 1. Be insightful. 2. Be philosophical. 3. Trust your guidance. If this sounds somewhat heady, it is only because serendipity, at this point, eases for a moment into a scholarly field. You see, probability is chance intellectualized. To convince yourself of this you need only look at a dictionary definition of probability. It says, "Probability: the likelihood of the occurrence of any particular form of an event, estimated as the ratio of the number of ways in which that form might occur to the whole number of ways in which the event might occur in any form."

Whatever you may think of that, for our purpose probability is simply a chance happening, and a chance happening is an adventure in serendipity, and we can go on from here to our first point: Be insightful!

The Princes of Serendip made it clear that when a chance happening or an unusual probability runs into you, or you into it, it is like unexpectedly finding a coin. Pick it up. Look it over. See whether it is genuine or counterfeit. Look it over again. Never throw it away without a thoroughgoing, exhaustive examination. *Be insightful.*

Our most familiar example of insightfulness in the case of a probability is, of course, the discovery of penicillin. By now it is fairly well known that on a May afternoon in 1928, a Scottish bacteriologist, working at St. Mary's Hospital in London, reexamined some of his early culture plates. By chance he noticed that one of the mold spores had produced an unusual effect. It had "spoiled." Many an investigator in the past had no doubt observed the very same phenomenon on other plates and thrown them away, seeing in them only a bad coin, a contaminated specimen.

The ratio of probability that this particular mold would be examined more closely was something like five hundred to one, but bacteriologist Alexander Fleming was Scotch. He was also serendipitous. He gave the mold a second glance.

Putting the plate under strong magnification, he noticed

that the culture of pus-producing bacteria dissolved when in contact with the mold. When he put the mold in a growth-producing broth, he found that from the mold there passed a substance so powerful that it stopped a small army of disease-producing germs dead in their tracks.

This was the discovery responsible for the development of penicillin. This was the probability that opened doors on a whole new and teeming field of antibiotics which gave rise to a multibillion-dollar industry, all because a Scotsman took a studied look into his microscopic lens.

Be insightful! You may be the chosen one for an equally great discovery in your time!

Secondly, by all means: *Be philosophical!*

Many were the times that the wayfaring Princes of Serendip ran into things that did not immediately "pay off." This becomes especially clear when we remember that the princes were, after all, sons of a king, and their ultimate goal was, of course, their father's kingdom. Yet along the many miles and years of their sojourn in a foreign land, the resource that sustained them was their outlook on life. Every event had meaning for them even though the meaning was not immediately clear. This was a great philosophical discovery.

A man in Königsberg, Germany, whose name was Immanuel Kant, put it this way: "Accept all of your duties as divine commands." That is a magnificent suggestion. It is not easy, but it is magnificent. If you have something that simply must be done, something that you cannot avoid doing, accept it as a "divine command," which is to say, approach it philosophically, joyfully, and with the best of good intentions.

Kant himself was a case in point. He was a small, hump-backed, puckish kind of man. Less than five feet tall, with a barrellike belly and a sunken chest, he tapped his way with a cane, head tilted to one side, one shoulder up and one shoulder down. As far as appearance was concerned, Kant had many things against him. Yet he approached his lot in life so philosophically that throughout his eighty years (1724-1804) he ruled the world of thought, and there is not a scholar today who can avoid the influence and challenge of the little giant of Königsberg: Out of the probability of failure and frustration, he forged success, and by a philosophy of life discovered God in man and man in God as few mortal men before or since his time have been able to do.

Think of the probabilities that were against Immanuel Kant. His parents were poor. Because they were Pietists and conscientious objectors they were out of favor with their time. Immanuel, named in honor of the Lord, was slated for the ministry. He never got to be a preacher, but he made his own spiritual discovery. God, he said, exists because man needs His existence. That was his serendipity experience. He never actually "found God" totally and convincingly, but he found many things that represented God, all the way from reason to faith. What is more, he combined faith with reason and left us a remarkable bit of philosophical advice. "Accept all of your duties as divine commands."

Trust your guidance. This is the third lesson to be learned from any case of probability, and I am tempted to give an illustration out of my own experience.

Following my college graduation in the Midwest I had the chance of jobs in both New York and Los Angeles. Both offers were equally secure (and risky), and both urged me to accept. Something within me strongly told me to take the job on the West Coast, though, rationally considered, the East Coast seemed somewhat the better of the two. I decided to flip a coin. Heads for California, tails for New

York. I tossed. It came up tails. Something told me it wasn't quite fair to flip just once, it should legitimately be two out of three. I tossed again. It came up heads. That was more like it! One for New York and one for California. I went into my third try. It was tails. New York it was. So I went to California.

I went to California because something deeper than coin-tossing assured me of a source of guidance that was not to be denied. Did I do right? Who is to say? All I know is that I have always felt rather good about trusting my guidance that day!

This is where serendipity comes in. Serendipity, according to my interpretation, insists that guidance is the inner prompting of an unshakable conviction. If the guidance is misty or morbid and needs the ESP of heads or tails, watch it. If it is wholesome, clear, and in the rhythm of your life, obey it. If it has a heavy touch, question it. If it has a light touch, follow it.

The serendipitous test of guidance is threefold: it always motivates you (you do not motivate it); it always fills you with a sense of rightness; it always leaves you and your world in better spirits than before.

Trust your guidance. Trust it as you trust your physical sense. Trust it as you trust your intuition. Among the built-in capabilities which we all spontaneously use and believe in, the sense of inner guidance must never be forgotten. Compared with the complexity of figuring out why you should do this or that, why you like a person or dislike him, why you should go here or there, the quiet eye of guidance sees and knows what the plodding, sluggish brain tries vainly to perceive.

Be insightful. Be philosophical. Trust your guidance. Chances are that in all probability you are what you are because of chance. Which is to say that chance is probably an important guidepost on the serendipity road where nothing happens without meaning, purpose, or the simple joy of traveling on in life.

4

THE SECRET OF CYCLES

I believe in laws—civil laws, natural laws, Karmic laws. I would like to change some of them, but I believe in them. Sometimes I am even tempted to believe in Murphy's Law.

Murphy's Law maintains that, "If anything can go wrong, it will." The reason I believe in this is because I also believe in Bach's Law which says, "If anything can go right, it must!"

The heart of Murphy's Law (and Bach's Law) is the premise that things move in cycles. Everything moves in cycles: the planets, the tide, the seasons, day and night. There are industrial cycles, political cycles, fashion cycles. Which brings us back to serendipity, the world where nothing is without meaning. Serendipity: an *unexpected* discovery of something worthwhile during a search for an *expected* something worthwhile. In the world of serendipity, chance is no longer chance; it may be the signature of God or good, and every experience is a guideline for a great adventure.

Serendipity alerts us to the fact that life, your life and mine, also moves in cycles. There are times when we should "lay low" and not force our luck, and there are times when we should "ride high" and take advantage of our good fortune. There is Murphy's Law, "If anything can go wrong, it will." And there is Bach's Law, "If anything can go right, it must!"

I like to think that the discovery of the wheel was a case of serendipity. Someone on his way to some distant goal happened to see a kid rolling a hoop or a stone or a log tumbling down a hill. Seeing this, he got to thinking. An inventive thought stirred in him and he said, "I'll make me a wheel!"

I like to think that I made an equally important serendipitous discovery when, in watching people roll the hoops of their ambitions or when I caught myself unexpectedly rolling down a hill, so to say, I decided that life is a wheel. Every last one of us has his ups and downs, his highs and lows, his top and bottom of the revolving wheel of life. But the new feature about my theory is that we cause the turning. We are responsible for what we call bright days and dark days, good breaks and bad, according to the thoughts we think, the attitudes we assume, and the way we look at things along the serendipity road. It is not a fickle fate that turns the wheel. We turn it.

These conclusions were confirmed by the experiences of the Princes of Serendip. Children of a king, heirs to a kingdom, they traveled the world in search of truth and found treasures to live by along the way. They did the turning. There was not a situation, act, event, or experience whose chain of circumstance did not lead right back to them, and that is how it is with us.

Now, of course, it often *seems* as if fate or destiny or some capricious prestidigitator is turning the wheel, but that is only because we do not think deeply enough or honestly enough or responsibly enough about our part in the scheme of things.

Consider the luck some people have at cards or any game of chance. Or games of skill, for that matter. We speak of "winning streaks," of "being on the ball," or "getting the breaks." We talk about having a "good cycle," or we say that life is doing us a "good turn." At such moments we can hardly lose. It is a mystery. It is beyond our rational explanation. If we try to analyze it we may destroy it. If we try to figure it out we may break the spell. It simply is the way it is, but the reason behind it is something in us. Something in us is causing the turning. We have caught on to some secret attunement. Usually at such times we are relaxed, receptive, inwardly confident. Even if we seem excited on the surface, at a subsurface level there is a most wonderful *knowing*. A partner has come into our life. We are in harmony with Bach's Law: "If anything can go right, it must!" How can we hold the harmony? Get synchronized with life's rhythm!

But life is a wheel. There could be a down cycle. We get out of rhythm. We find ourselves unsynchronized— out-of-sync, they call it. Something we did or thought, inadvertently or wittingly, starts the wheel turning and things begin to change.

Now we enter a time when luck cools and the good cards pass us by, being dealt to someone else. Fair enough. Life moves in cycles and for a time we may seem to have lost the magic touch. We are caught in Murphy's Law. But the Princes of Serendip insisted that even these periods are rich in lessons for good and growth if we are willing to see them through.

Let the down cycle be a time for learning. I caught on to this long ago on the road to maturity. Though I did not find maturity at once, I found things along the way that were fully as good. I learned that during the up cycle I should show *gratitude,* and on the down cycle I should demonstrate *patience,* and when the wheel seems still and scarcely moving I should be *both grateful and patient,* for these two are tremendous secrets along the serendipity road.

When I was a boy, my father was in the store business. He called it merchandising. He had a department store in Wisconsin and annually, in early January, he closed up shop for a week because of the winter cycle. Business was slow, the snow was high, and the store closed down. My father called it "inventory week," days when he and his sales force "took stock." This was also a period for redecorating and clearing away goods left over from the post-Christmas sales.

Inventory week was like a week of Sundays as far as our home life was concerned. My father was in a more relaxed, reflective, unhurried mood during these days. He took stock not only of the merchandise, but of himself, and I remember how our family used to sit together after supper and take an appraisal of ourselves. The impression on me was a lasting one and I suppose that is why I feel so strongly that life should definitely have its inventory cycle. In the business of living as in the business of merchandising, it is necessary to know where we stand and what resources we have that we can depend on.

Came the Depression and I remember how my father

said, "It will be a long cycle." It was. Murphy's Law was in the ascendancy. (Maybe because *everyone* was saying that it would be a long cycle!) But what I never forgot is that the wheel of life kept moving and that we were doing the turning. Our thoughts, our attitudes, our acts were and always are the governors of the wheel. Our state of consciousness is the hub. Sure enough, there came the day when the collective consciousness instituted another cycle and it seemed that if anything could go right, it would. And it did.

The big secret imparted by the Princes of Serendip is that the acres that lie fallow are not dead, they are restoring their energies. The earth covered by winter's cycle is renourishing itself. There is, as the wise man said, "For everyone . . . a season and a time for every matter under heaven." Even more wisely he added, "That which is to be, already has been; and God seeks what has been driven away."

There are times when it may be best to "close the store," and there are periods when it is wise to open wide the doors. If there is anything to Murphy's Law, which says, "If something can go wrong, it will," then it must follow as day follows night that there definitely is something to Bach's Law, which says, "If anything can go right, it must!"

5

ACCEPTING
THE UNEXPECTED

*E*very once in a while I run into situations which bear the unmistakable tag, "Accidentally yours." My life is linked with such events and I am beginning to believe, as did the Princes of Serendip, that these occurrences may be "guidemen in disguise."

There was, for example, my one and only serious auto accident, when I was in my teens. It was snowing on the Wisconsin hill on that bleak December night. I was hurrying home for the Christmas holidays. The convertible skidded, struck a culvert, caromed into the air and tossed me into a stubble-field where I lay covered with sleet and snow. An hour later when I "came to," when I stood up dazed and dizzy and saw the canvas top of the convertible draped over a barbed-wire fence and the car standing unsteadily on its twisted wheels, I counted it a tragedy.

Today as I look back on that mishap or see the scars still visible on my right leg, I realize that this was the most persuasive lesson in driving I ever had. Never again have I been that reckless. I learned a great deal more from that winter's night than from any driver's test or traffic experience. Not that I am recommending this kind of a course; I am merely saying that something was salvaged from this pre-Christmas encounter, a gift-wrapped package clearly marked, "Accidentally yours."

But what if I had been injured seriously? Then I would have to write the story from *that* standpoint. Who is to say what the badly injured say as they look back, and who can report for the dead excepting those who have had the experience? Every event of this kind has meaning beyond our first impression and significance far greater than we know. Accidents bring us face to face with "guide-men in disguise." So said the Princes of Serendip, and so say I.

Following this line of reasoning, we can find some provocative insights when we reflect upon the unexpected. I now realize that the car accident gave me a special sense of destiny. Even today I feel that I was spared for a purpose, and I come around to the conclusion that everything in life has an over-meaning. If the *Something* that spared me had me under its watchful eye during that nocturnal rendezvous, then *every* occasion takes on more significance. Then all of life is raised an octave and every moment becomes richer and more important in the scheme of things.

One of the most important lessons out of the world of serendipity is at this very point: every experience is a reminder that nothing is irrelevant. There is an "Unknown-Knower" behind everything that happens.

Eventually we learn that in life there are no missing links. To live this way and think this way immediately sets our journey on a higher road. Some people refer to this Unknown-Knower as God. Others think in terms of guardian angels, or the working of a causal law. For the Princes of Serendip the analogy was "guide-men in disguise," probably because they lived in the Arabian Nights country where things were given a romantic, highly imaginative touch. But in all countries and in all cultures, it is a great discovery to learn the meaning of "Accidentally yours."

Recently I was in Iran. I wanted to see the spot in Tabriz where the forerunner of the Baha'i faith, a young man nicknamed "the Bab," was executed a hundred and more years ago. The Bab had a saying, "I will not die until my mission in life has been fulfilled." Came the day when he was seized by the authorities and sentenced to death for subversive activities and stirring up the people.

He was suspended by his wrists from a crossbar in the city square. A firing squad leveled forty loaded rifles at him, but when the smoke cleared, there stood the Bab uninjured on the ground. The bullets had merely severed the thongs that had bound him. The officials called it an accident. His followers hailed it as a miracle. The Bab said that God had spared him in order that he might fulfill his mission, and only after he had attended to his unfinished business was he apprehended and executed.

Such thinking and such faith are primarily a way of life rather than a creed. They represent a point of view that cannot be reduced totally to reason or logic. "Accidentally yours" may be one way of saying that God has a special job and mission for you and that is why you are still around.

I have a hunch that the "guide-men in disguise" may represent some deep-seated personal motivation which the world of serendipity brings into focus and expression. It has long been a theory of mine that every person has some specific talent or aptitude in which he excels, if he can but discover what it is. There's the rub. Consider how long some people go through life before they discover that secret proficiency. Some never discover it. But the fact is that unexpected encounters and the unforeseen may be trigger-points which release or uncover these capabilities.

One of the most remarkable instances was the case of one Johannes Briggs, who had the extreme misfortune of losing both legs and a hand. Out of this extremity he detected that he had phenomenal dexterity in the hand that remained. Developing this, he became one of Europe's most renowned prestidigitators, and punsters are still saying that in the realm of magic the name of Johannes Briggs is one to conjure with.

But you need not go into the past or search out such extreme cases to find examples of how the unexpected brings out new talents and unlocks some greater good. I found a case in point the other day when, for the first time, I met Dr. J. Allen Hynek, head of the astronomy department at Northwestern University and long-time consultant to the Air Force on Unidentified Flying Objects. Because of my long interest in UFO's and my respect for what the National Investigations Committee on Aerial Phenomena has so ably done for many years, I had been disconcerted by Dr. Hynek's erstwhile statement that the Hillsdale, Michigan, sightings were due to "swamp gas." In fact, this story was so widely circulated that Hynek's name became synonymous with thoughtless debunkers of the entire UFO story.

Upon meeting Dr. Hynek I realized how his viewpoint had changed, and how in walking the serendipity road he had encountered so many sane and sober people who reported sightings that he discovered within himself a sudden will to investigate this whole field in depth from both the scientific and the psychological approach. What was more, I discovered (and others who knew Dr. Hynek confirmed the opinion) that here was a man who had an empathy with people that neither the press nor he himself had ever fully detected. This, of course, may have come from living overly much in an ivory tower. At any rate, far from discounting these phenomena as "swamp gas," this particular scientist courageously requested reports from anyone and everyone who may have seen or who thinks he has seen a UFO. Whether "flying saucers" exist or not, one never knows where the "guide-men in disguise" will lead you next.

An even closer-to-home illustration comes to mind. Shortly after we were married, my wife Lorena decided to complete her college work in home economics. Her thesis assignment was "The Nutritive and Protein Value of Soybeans as a Meat Substitute," and for this dissertation she had soybean sprouts in boxes and tins all over the house. Then came the preparation of soybean dishes, many of which were tested on me but most of which were artistically prepared for serving in the university's home economics department.

Lorena was never completely sold on the nutritional field as a career, but since she had started she was determined to see it through. One aesthetic feature bothered her. Some of the soybean creations she cooked up were so colorful and artistic that it gave her a sinking feeling whenever she saw them devoured by hungry guests! All she had left was a detailed description of how they were prepared and how they looked.

One day when she was hurrying from the classroom she literally bumped head-on into a photographer from *Life* magazine, who was on campus doing a documentary on college housing. The photographer was Margaret Bourke-White. After recovering from the physical encounter, the visiting camerawoman said: "Well, you come as if called. Why don't you help me while I'm here on my assignment?" Lorena did, even though it was nothing more than the menial task of carrying the flash equipment and serving as campus guide.

Out of this association, however, came an idea. It flashed into Lorena's mind that if she had a camera she could get a picture record of her soybean dishes and have them for time and eternity, even after they had been gobbled up by admiring diners. She borrowed some camera equipment from the photographic department and set to work. With her first attempt she discovered that she had not only an aptitude but a passion for photography, which outreached her interest in foods. The unexpected run-in in a classroom corridor did the trick and Lorena went on to win a number of national awards—not in foods but in photos.

"Guide-men in disguise" are apparently waiting just around the corners of life. They challenge us to accept the unexpected, or at least to pause to analyze what these unlooked-for happenings may mean in relation to the total business of living. How far or how meaningful we wish to make them is up to us. Some people who have the courage to investigate them down to their deepest depths come up with the conclusion that all are links in a meaningful chain, even those situations which carry the unmistakable tag, "Accidentally yours."

6
THE CREDIBILITY
OF THE INCREDIBLE

*I*n the early days of sound recorders I had an instrument that recorded on wire. It was phenomenal how the thin-as-silk thread of steel wire accomplished its job, picking up the strains of symphonies, the roar of locomotives, or the singing of a bird.

One day I interviewed an Amishman whose stolid, bearded face belied any interest in these modern miracles. He was ungiven to emotion. When I played back my interview with him so that he could hear the magic of the wire, I said, "Isn't it wonderful? Every word comes back exactly as you said it!" He never changed expression. Instead he shrugged and said, "It would be more wonderful if what I said came back *different*."

That hit me with the credibility of the incredible. To be sure, it is remarkable that you can record a rock 'n' roll tune on wire or tape, but it would indeed be more remarkable if, in playing it back, out came a Bach sonata. It is amazing to think of a tiny acorn giving rise to a giant oak, but if it turned out to be a weeping willow, what then? Or take the matter of cosmic affairs. It is incredible how the planets just hang there in outer space, tracing their courses, keeping their orbits, maintaining a most complicated, split-second schedule through endless time. But if some morning the sun did *not* come up, that would be even more incredible!

All of which brings me to the wonderful world of serendipity. The three Princes of Serendip, soldiers of fortune that they were, had a few irrefutable convictions up their embroidered sleeves. One was this: *There is a law!* What you put on a tape will come back to you as recorded. What you sow, you will reap. The forces of nature which seem incredible would be truly incredible if they ever ceased to demonstrate their credibility.

So when the Princes were asked to tell fortunes, as they often were, and when they were requested to counsel people, they usually held a conference. They got their heads together and said, "Let's figure this out on the basis of credibility."

For example, one day a woman came to them and said, "Will I be lucky in love?"

The Princes went into a huddle. One of their secrets was that they had an uncanny record of everyone who came to them, and their mental filing system was a wonder to behold. Here they were, a thousand years before computers and memory banks, but they had a data system all their own. When they processed the information on their woman client, they realized that for twenty years (she was now thirty-nine) she had been saying to herself, "Unlucky in love! I am lucky in everything else, but unlucky in love."

Since the Princes knew how deeply this had become embedded in the woman's consciousness, they said, "Sorry, but we see no change in your destiny."

"Incredible!" exclaimed the woman.

"Credible," said the Princes, as if they still had their ears to the tape of this woman's recorded life.

One of the most amazing twists of incredibility is what men will do with this law (divine law) in order to create a credibility gap. This, in the world of serendipity, is incomprehensible. The idea that truth can be perverted into falsehood and be expected to serve a constructive need is, according to the Princes of Serendip, a denial of the law.

There was a king in an ancient country called Talamira who insisted that he had the right to manipulate truth as it suited his needs. He said, in effect, that the end justified the means and that what the people did not know did not hurt them.

One day his spies infiltrated a neighboring kingdom, Anasmania. They wore disguises, they had learned the Anasmanian language, and they might never have been caught but for the fact that they had not learned to count as the people counted in Anasmania. In this land whenever the inhabitants counted money or cattle or anything of any kind, they always began with "zero" instead of "one." This was to show that there is such a thing as nothing. A man would count his prayer beads in Anasmania by first showing his empty hands and saying, "zero." Then he would begin his, "one, two, three."

The spies from Talamira had overlooked this simple custom. When paying their bill at an inn they promptly began with "one, two, three." This made the innkeeper suspicious; he called the authorities and the men were arrested.

When the King of Talamira heard of this he immediately issued a statement saying that his men had been abducted while walking quietly along the borders of their own country. This, of course, was untrue, but he went even further and warned the ruler of Anasmania that if the men were not released immediately they would be freed by force. It was all quite incredible.

Time dragged on and with each passing day the gap between truth and fiction widened until, to the humility of both the king and the subjects of Talamira, the king had to admit that he had not told the truth. Not only did he lose face, he had to give the ruler of Anasmania twelve teams of pure-white oxen for the spies' release.

This sort of thing goes on in all countries and there is good evidence that it happens in most families, businesses, and in political and social circles as well. It is quite incredible because

> *There is a law,*
> *you cannot beat it;*
> *It rests on truth,*
> *you cannot unseat it.*
> *You cannot build a bridge*
> *sufficiently strong,*
> *To span the credibility gap*
> *for long.*

Of course, these are truths you run into most frequently only in the world of serendipity.

Not long ago a story appeared in the press telling about a sixteen-year-old boy from Bishop, Texas, named Mark Whitaker who discovered a new comet. Think of that! Here you have observatories all over the world. Huge observatories. Mt. Wilson, with a 100-inch telescope. Mt. Palomar, with a 200-inch telescope made out of a single block of Pyrex glass which required ten years to parabolize the surface.

Mark Whitaker had a home-made telescope that measured just four inches and cost him seven dollars and fifty cents.

One night, his third night of peering through this self-constructed instrument, he sat up until 2 a.m. and spotted something in the heavens. The next night he traced the object again, and on the third night he telephoned the Harvard Observatory. The men there said, "Try the Smithsonian Astrophysical Observatory and see what they have to say."

Mark called them up. "I think I've found a new comet," he said. "I don't know if it's new or periodic. It doesn't have a tail."

It was absolutely incredible. Or was it?

The Smithsonian Observatory and the Lowell Observatory of Flagstaff, Arizona, confirmed Mark's report and named the comet Whitaker-Thomas, adding to Mark's name the name of a professional astronomer who helped in the confirmation.

There is a law. It says that if you engage in a skywatch you may see something. It does not say that you *will* see something, but that you *might*. And that is the marvel of life's entire adventure. That, in fact, is the secret of the credibility of the incredible, and it applies whether you are in the observatory on Mt. Palomar or in your own backyard looking hopefully at the stars.

The credibility of the incredible leads us directly into the matter of prophecies and prognostications. It sparks the age-old question: can predictions really be made about coming events? Is the future already sketched out and are there individuals who can read the signs in their crystal balls?

Serendipity has an answer. It says, "God foreknows but He does not foreordain." Now this may run contrary to what some theologians believe and it may create all sorts of arguments in various schools of thought, but if I read the world of serendipity aright, it puts the issue squarely up to each individual. God, like a wise parent, knows what the actions of His children will lead to but He does not foreordain these actions. His foresight, unbounded by the limited dimensions that bind us humans, is omniscient, but He is not a puppeteer who has us on His strings.

But are there people who can foretell and predict what will happen?

Serendipity has the answer. It suggests that *insight into God's law and a study of man's life are reasonable standards by which future events can be predicted*. It also warns us that the predictions are by no means infallible because the predictor is himself bound by the standards. Most modern seers (so-called) and fortune-tellers and self-styled prophets are less than fifty percent right in their pronouncements. This means that they are more than fifty percent wrong. Like the various polls and public-opinion tabulations they can be completely wrong, and like the stock-market analysts they can be tragically incorrect.

Before the financial crash that ushered in the great depression of the 1930's many an expert said it would be a "temporary recession." It was a long one; it lasted twelve years. In the field of religion there have been predictions about the "end of the world" ever since man first roamed the earth. The earth still stands. In the realm of prophecy there have been endless warnings that a good portion of California will drop into the sea. Nothing significant has happened, though everyone knows about the San Andreas fault.

St. John on the Isle of Patmos foretold startling events

which some religionists feel point to things that will come to pass in our day; but each age and each generation have insisted that these things would happen in *their* time.

There *were* predictions by the Oracle at Delphi, some of which came true (less than twenty percent). Many were ambiguous. For example, when the Oracle said, "The Greeks the Romans will destroy," did she mean that the Romans would destroy the Greeks or the Greeks the Romans?

Then there was Nostradamus. This sixteenth-century French astrologer wrote a lengthy prophecy in rhyme and his devotees believe that some of his sayings came to pass. Such was also the case with the seventeenth-century prophetess Mother Shipton. And there are those who believe there were and are seers and soothsayers in our century, modern prophets such as Edgar Cayce, Betty Ritter, Jeane Dixon.

It is all highly fascinating and dramatic, and if we believe in retrocognition should we not logically believe in precognition? After all, who among us has not had hunches that came true, or feelings that materialized, or dreams that were confirmed by unfolding events? Who does not believe in the law of probabilities or coincidences, or in the interpenetration of moments of ESP? Or who would want to live in a universe that does not have these overtones or that fails to excite us with the speculation of the great unknown?

But in the wonderful world of serendipity we stand on ground more solid than that of divination or crystal gazing. The Princes of Serendip (symbols of those who walk insightfully) had a deep-seated belief that if we know God's law and have a knowledge of the true nature of a man, it may be possible to foretell what could conceivably come to pass in that man's life. In fact, the Princes were so sure of the equation of God's-law-in-man's-conduct that they used it as a formula in their interpretation of people whom they met along the way.

When you and I turn this mirror of reflection upon ourselves we, too, may be able to divine the credibility of the incredible and catch a hint of our future as it emerges out of your life and mine.

7

MIRACLES ARE
WHERE YOU FIND THEM

$\mathcal{T}$he world of serendipity is a subtle world. Those who catch on to its secrets become princes—princes of Serendip. They see things in a new light. Like the original Princes of Serendip who left their father's house to make their journey in uncharted lands, they know that some day they will be back on the grounds of the kingdom. In fact, one of their secrets is that in all their journeying they never forget who and what they are. They carry the kingdom's secret with them.

This awareness gives an amazingly rich insight to their life, combining a light touch with a solid perspective, an unbeatable combination for the integrated life.

Take the matter of so-called miracles. Often in their traveling, the Princes were beset by excited people who claimed they had encountered a "supernatural" happening. The Princes took it all in stride with a "maybe yes, maybe no" attitude. Never intolerant, never too gullible, their marvelous balance imparted balance to others along the way.

I thought of this recently when I went to the Philippines. I was in the world of serendipity the moment I stepped into the cab at the Manila airport. The driver, young, eager-eyed, with a running knowledge of English, had the statue of a saint magnetized to the cab's dashboard. He was pleased when I identified it as St. Anthony, a favorite of mine, and it was this common ground that caused Marcelo to be at my beck and call during my island stay.

"If you ever hear of any miracles," I told him as he drove Lorena (Mrs. Bach) and me to our hotel, "I'd be interested."

"There is one right now!" he exclaimed, his dark eyes dancing. "Up in Catarman!"

"What kind of a miracle?"

"Mushrooms!" he cried.

Taxi drivers all over the world will take you just about anywhere to see just about anything, for a price, and Marcelo was no exception. But he had an undying penchant for miracles and a will to believe that I almost envied. So, with the Princes of Serendip in mind, and never knowing just what we might run into, we set the taxi meter for Catarman.

Now it was true that near the warehouse of Bruno Tiberio on Jacinto Street in Catarman, Samar, huge mushrooms were ambitiously growing. They measured from six to ten inches in diameter and the Tiberios had been picking them daily for several weeks. Covering a patch of some twenty square feet, they had sprung up unplanted and unannounced in fantastic abundance in sidewalk cracks and along the warehouse's concrete wall.

Bruno Tiberio was having a difficult time keeping the people from running off with his crop, especially since the variety was edible. There had never been anything unusual about his warehouse until a typhoon hit Catarman some six months ago. One morning when Senor Tiberio went to work he saw the place strewn with what looked like manna from heaven. The miracle mushrooms had come.

Bruno discovered that all they needed was water and some tender loving care. He could have made a big religious thing out of it, but he didn't. Not yet, at least. One reason was that three kilometers from Catarman, in Barrio Cawayan, a patch of miracle squash had also sprung up unannounced after the typhoon had spent its strength.

"There may be ways of explaining these phenomena," said Dr. O. J. Villaver, supervisor of the Bureau of Animal Industry, "but if some people want to call them miracles, that is fine with me."

That, it seemed to me, was worthy of the Princes of Serendip. Marcelo, however, was disappointed. He did not like it that in the world of serendipity there are people who see both sides of a question. He was even more put out when I dropped around to the headquarters of the *Iglesia Ni Cristo*, a viable religious movement that has caught the imagination and loyalties of thousands of Filipinos who either had no church home or who were defecting from the Catholic Church and following the apocalyptic message of one Felix Manalo (whom the *Iglesia* insists is the "final infallible Messenger of God").

What did the *Iglesia* think of the mushrooms and the squash and "miracles" in general? Utter nonsense, the authorities told me. They cited the famous "Miracle of the

Virgin in Cabra Island," where hundreds of people claimed they saw a vision of the Virgin Mary. They cued me in on the "showers of rose petals" that were supposed to have been seen by the credulous in Lipa City. Utter nonsense, they repeated. But I could almost hear the Princes of Serendip say, "Now, let's not be too hasty. Maybe some people *do* see things, or need to see them."

Then something happened. Early one morning Marcelo, bursting with excitement, reported that a new miracle had just happened in Caloocan, a Manila suburb. A statue of the Infant Jesus of Prague had miraculously begun to weep tears of blood.

Carried away by Marcelo's enthusiasm, even Lorena got excited, especially when she learned that photographers who had tried to take pictures of the statue discovered that their flash bulbs would not go off and that their films were spoiled. Lorena's photographic skill accepted this as a direct challenge. She loaded her Leica and her Nikon, checked her flash equipment, and off we went.

Caloocan City, ten kilometers from the heart of Manila, had chuckholed streets, cheap wooden shops, and the crowded traffic barely allowed our mini-taxi to maneuver its way to the place of the miracle, Villa Maria Street. The narrow thoroughfare was jammed with people. Young and old, devotee and curious were converging on a humble two-story wooden house, the home of the weeping *Nino*. The faithful were bringing flowers and candles. An enterprising vendor had set up a soft drink stall nearby. There was holiday excitement in the air.

At the sight of the battery of cameras strung around Lorena's neck, friendly people made way for us to get into the house. The twelve-foot-square room was jam-packed. Antonio Ortega, about twenty-five and amazingly calm, was asserting himself as head of the house by tacking up a sign:

IWASAN ANG PAGBIGAY NG ABULOY. This is the Tagalog way of saying, "Please do not give us any donations." In the light of the apparent need in this household, this declaration would have pleased the Princes of Serendip immensely. Surely they would have agreed that this attested to the sincerity of the situation.

Antonio Ortega was more than courteous. He asked the crowd to stand aside so that we could get a good look at the statue, a two-foot-high ceramic of an Infant standing, kingly crown on head, holding in its left hand a small globe and cross. This robed figure was securely encased in glass and had apparently not been tampered with. The "tears of blood"? On close inspection, Marcelo and I concluded that there were indeed some drops, red in color, streaking the cheeks and staining the statue's white satin dress. Reverently Marcelo made the sign of the cross.

According to Ortega, the statue had been in the parental family for thirty years and had been handed down to him from his grandparents. Had there ever been anything unusual about it before? Three years ago he had noticed that the left eye of the image seemed to open and close. He had kept this fact jealously to himself.

While he told me these things, Lorena took pictures of the statue both by flash and with available light. Later we were to see that her technique had apparently been more productive than that reported by earlier photographers. Her pictures did turn out remarkably bright, but showed no tears.

Antonio Ortega confided to me that the dress worn by the Infant had been made by Antonio's wife. Shortly before the "miracle of the tears," Antonio and his wife had a heated argument over family affairs and there was now talk of separation. In fact, she had packed up and left about a week ago. Then the Infant began to weep, he said.

There was a chance that the tears would bring a reconciliation.

Suddenly, while we were talking, someone in the room shouted, "It's weeping again!" There was a great surge of the crowd. Marcelo made the sign of the cross. The cry was repeated, but as I worked my way to the glass case there were definitely no "fresh tears" (at least I did not see any; Marcelo said he did and it can certainly be argued that he saw what I did not see).

I had to remind myself that in the world of serendipity there is the inner awareness that there *is* something beyond the "natural" and higher than the "normal" which justifies and corroborates our instances of extrasensory and divine attunement. With guarded caution the Princes of Serendip always looked both ways, to the phenomenal no less than to the unseen realities of life. Had the statue wept? Or could the so-called tears have been caused by condensation inside the case? Did it cry or had someone tampered with the image?

The questions, like the quest, are endless. A miracle, according to Marcelo, is a miracle. To which I could only add that it exists in the consciousness of the believer. With which we made our way to the car, while the faithful continued bringing flowers and candles and cakes as if a miracle had already taken place in their hearts.

When the Princes of Serendip encountered things that seemed unusual and strange, they saw in them the unspeakable wonder of a world where nothing is absolutely final and few things are irrevocably fixed. The adventure is in the quest, the joy is in the journey, and something deeply reminiscent of the kingdom dwells in every heart.

The spark of faith, the fire of doubt, the wish to believe, the will to question, the marvel, mystery, magic, are telltale signs along the way while all of us, true princes of

Serendip, pursue the course beckoned by the lure of life. As for miracles, they are where you find them. Are they real? Maybe yes, maybe no. It is well to remember what the Princes often said: "The greatest miracle of all is the simple fact of *being*, and of being as best you can your truest self."

8
WHO IS YOUR GSF?

*D*uring my elementary-school days I had an English teacher who believed in creative education. She had her own system of visual aids. When we were introduced to Coleridge's "Ancient Mariner," she appeared in class with a homemade albatross around her neck. On another occasion she helped us remember Schiller's "William Tell" by demonstrating how difficult it is to balance an apple on one's head. And one day she wrote on the blackboard in her best Spencerian hand, "Who is your GSF?"

We knew this was a teaser for our next assignment, and it started us thinking. For several days we greeted each other with the words, "Who is your GSF?" (having no idea what we were saying). Then she tacked a large sketch of Nathaniel Hawthorne on the wall and let us look at the visage of this bronzed New Englander until his solemnity got through to us. It was only after she told us about the man, his writings, and his career, that she gave us the meaning of "GSF." It was her alphabetized abbreviation for the "Great Stone Face," to her one of Hawthorne's most imaginative works.

Nowadays when our abecedarians have forced us to think in terms of acronyms, we all know what CIA, GOP, FBI, DAR, LSD, AAA, and all the rest stand for. But one combination, learned many years ago, still takes precedence in my mind over all the rest: GSF.

Although he was probably unaware of it, Nathaniel Hawthorne was an out-and-out serendipitist. He presented a thesis in his "Great Stone Face" with which the Princes of Serendip would have agreed unanimously: *The thing you set your mind on is the thing you ultimately become.* In fact, there is more to it than that. You take on the qualities and characteristics of the people and things with whom you associate, and something of you rubs off on them. These are definitely fundamental principles of serendipity.

As I have said, Hawthorne may not have been aware of his serendipitous leanings, because his goal was so rigidly moralistic. Coming as he did of solid, grave-faced, long-coated Puritan stock, he struggled all his life with the problem of sin and suffering. Life to him was serious business and he felt alone and aloof up there in his ivory-tower world. Emerson, his contemporary, tried to cheer him up with a philosophy of light and joy, but Hawthorne had his heart set on solving the solemn mystery of good and evil. He never solved it, but along the way he made other marvelous discoveries which were just as rewarding as the goal he sought and did not find. This, of course, is the essence of serendipity.

The story of the Great Stone Face is familiar to most Americans of the establishment (and not unfamiliar to Americans of the dis-establishment as well). They know that Hawthorne was enchanted by a rocky profile in the White Mountains of New Hampshire, a stony formation in the Franconia range known as "The Old Man of the Mountain." When viewed from a certain angle the "Old Man" became a compelling figure. He still does. So does Hawthorne. So does everyone when viewed from the right perspective.

Nathaniel never forgot the vivid impression this profile made on him during his boyhood. So he wrote the story of a youngster who dreams that some day the living replica of the Great Stone Face will appear. The boy hopes to live and see the day. The years pass. The dream persists. The boy grows to manhood. Still the stranger does not come. Eventually the dreamer realizes that he himself bears the image and the features of the object of his dream. *He* is the Great Stone Face.

I can see the Princes of Serendip guiding the author's hand in this tender story. Hawthorne had political ambitions and for a time was the American consul in Liverpool, but the serendipity road had many unexpected twists and turns for him. The world never thinks. of him as a statesman, preferring to remember him for his literary works. His books—*The Scarlet Letter, The Marble Faun, The House of Seven Gables*, and the story "The Great Stone Face"—and not politics represented his deepest desires. The goal he thought he wanted, a governmental career, was not the goal he carried in his heart. Whenever he met people he was instinctively writing stories about them, seeing them, so he thought, through God's eyes. The thing he set his mind on was the thing he became. He took on the qualities and characteristics of the places and people with whom he associated, and something of Hawthorne rubbed off on them.

The Princes of Serendip could also have had political aspirations. After all, they were sons of a king. But, suspicious of affairs of state and not wishing to interfere with their father's rule, they went a-wandering. I think they would have understood the serendipitous features of our mangled presidential campaigns in which voters become increasingly more like the candidates they champion. In fact, some years ago they might have seen a parallel between Eugene McCarthy and the Great Stone Face.

McCarthy did not reach his goal of becoming president but some equally important things happened to him along the way. He discovered that his impact on a segment of Americans far surpassed his expectations. Young people caught on to his nonpolitical approach to politics. A new image of the political system took shape. McCarthy spoke like a poet, gave counsel like a professor, and gathered his young followers under his wing with fatherly affection. For many young Americans, McCarthy became their GSF.

Some McCarthy enthusiasts got out of hand, to be sure, but certain others shaved their beards, dressed more conventionally, and took a more reflective view on politics and life. The McCarthy profile which they had watched and studied for so long could now be recognized within themselves. His sincerity, idealism, and conviction that he had to "do his thing" no matter if it cost him the election, were qualities many of his youthful adherents embraced and reflected in themselves. For a time, he was their GSF. *The thing we set our minds on is the thing we ultimately become.*

Our highly analytic age has even brought this thesis down

to dogs. We become not only like the dreams we dream or like the people with whom we associate, we also take on the characteristics of our pets, and they in turn begin to be like us. We choose our dogs, cats, and pet birds in keeping with some canine, feline, or ornithological trait that slumbers deep within us.

There is the bulldog-type person and the dachshund-type. There is the Angora-cat individual and the myna-bird person. There are those who have lions for pets because of their own leonine qualities, and there are those who have panthers, falcons, peacocks, turtles, rabbits, even skinks and skunks, for reasons of personal identification. (Incidentally, skunks have some commendable qualities—gentleness, for example—to offset their odoriferous trademark.) More and more we begin to resemble the things with which we live and they, in turn, take on our qualities.

As a boy I had a collie because of its docile nature and its tendency to obedience. These were also my personal traits. As a young man I turned to wire-haired terriers. They were the hippie type, representing something in me that I was afraid to express because of my puritanical orientation, like Hawthorne's. Then I went through the spitz and boxer stages, which reflected my resistance to "freedom on a leash." Currently I am all for schnauzers, who are known as "little people." They are docile and obedient. I am getting more and more like my schnauzer and he is getting all too much like me.

If you plan to be a businessman, associate with people successful in business. If your ambition is to be a musician, get to know accomplished people in music. If you want to excel in anything, get with those who live, think, love, and work in that field. But heed a serendipitous warning: read people aright and be sure they are what they represent themselves to be.

In this connection there is the serendipitous story of Harpocrates, a mythological character who was revered as the god of silence. People in great numbers came to worship at his shrine and the finest artisans in Rome and Athens made statues of him. He was represented as a youthful figure proudly standing with his index finger in his mouth—the god of silence.

Gradually it dawned on his worshipers that their adoration of him was getting them nowhere. It was merely taking up their valuable time, for they would spend long hours in front of the god's statue with their index fingers in their mouths, too. Finally a learned scholar did some research on Harpocrates and discovered he was really not a god at all. He was actually the sculptured figure of a young man who had never gotten over sucking his thumb.

The Princes of Serendip would have seen through Harpocrates immediately. Instead of reasoning from the universal premises glibly accepted by the masses, they reasoned from experience of the natural order of things, penetrating through the symbols into the actual, unadulterated life of the individual.

One should give serious thought to the thing he chooses as his object of worship and to the person he selects as his GSF. Be careful in selecting your guru or your roommate or even your psychiatrist, for that matter. Serendipity has a saying, "Be wary whom you marry." Obviously you must use your own judgment in deciding how far you wish to go in this counsel, but remember that you do become like those with whom you spend your life and something of you rubs off on them. Two people intimately involved over a period of time not only take on each other's attitudes, they begin to look alike and talk alike and think alike.

It would be interesting to know what the Princes of Serendip would have said about the electronic matchmaking machines which are designed to bring the right boy-girl combination together, even down to the proper blood types and chromosomes. "For $15," say the ads, "we will help you find your perfect mate. You will receive a complete set of seven (7) partner-types scientifically selected for you to date. Date them and take your choice. Our happy, satisfied couples are your best guarantee. Our service provides values, opinions, characteristics, and all other details assuring you the perfect match! Let the electronic matchmaker work for *you*!"

When you look for the perfect partner (or for the Great Stone Face, for that matter) through the megaloptic eyes of a computer, you have, of course, injected a new viewpoint into the world of serendipity. But the principle remains the same: *The thing you set your mind on is the thing you become.*

I suppose that is why (computers notwithstanding) the three Princes of Serendip suggested that we choose our friends as we do our food: carefully. Beware of those that are over-processed! Be cautious of foods (and friends) that hint of spoilage. Watch out for those that are overdone, unless your constitution is sufficiently strong to digest them thoroughly.

Give those that are on sale, both friends and foods, special inspection. Are they tree-ripened or windfalls? Were they picked prematurely? Are they overly refrigerated or dehydrated? How did they stand the crating and the shipping and the changes in temperature? Are they too soft, too hard, too fresh, too stale, too sweet, too sour? And remember that you cannot always tell merely by appearances. A slightly shriveled berry may have the loveliest taste, while a lovely-looking melon may be rotten at the center. Or consider the mushroom!

Whether it is an image in a mountain like Hawthorne's

Great Stone Face, or a dog or cat or any other pet, or a partner in life, or even food, something in them all becomes a part of us.

By the way, who is *your* GSF?

9

NEVER ON BROADWAY

*W*hen you turn the mirror of reflection on yourself, when you look yourself in the eye and ask, "What great goal in life have I never reached?" what is your answer?

What have you missed (or what has missed you) that you had your heart set on? What target have you been shooting at, hitting all the perimeter circles but not the bull's-eye? Where do you still want to go that you have never been, or what do you still want to get that you have never gotten?

In the quiet of my study the other day I addressed the question to myself, "What has been your unreached goal?" A number of things sprang to mind. Some of them had been stilled by the years, several had been sublimated, some were still on the agenda. But the question persisted, "What great goal has eluded you?"

I had to confess that a major unrealized dream was my lifelong ambition to get a play on Broadway. Ever since my earliest work in playwriting, my efforts in theatre workshops, and my first full-length opus which enjoyed a successful university production, Broadway was my goal.

To think how close I came! There was the thirty-day run of my dramatic spectacle, "Light of Ages," in the Chicago Civic Opera House. There was the two-week showing of my play, "Mister Jim," at the Blackstone Theatre in Chicago. There was the stage production of a play of mine at St. Regis College, Denver. There was "Within These Walls," scheduled for a New York production even to the point where the wardrobe had been ordered and publicity was in the works, when it was called off. "Too controversially religious," said the previewers! I had a play produced in a showcase theatre in Hollywood and in Philadelphia. All this, but never on Broadway.

I discussed this situation in mental conferences with the Princes of Serendip and they gave me some enlightening insights.

"You see," they explained, "but for the fact that you had your eye on Broadway you might never have done as well in the less-than-Broadway productions. In hoping for New York you *did* have success on the streets of hometown. The goals realized often justify the unreached goal."

That was one way of looking at things even though it was by no means satisfying. Then the Princes made another serendipitous observation. "To realize Broadway as a goal," they said, "you must set a goal beyond

Broadway. In order to reach a certain height, you must overreach it. To jump a given distance, you must have the ability to overjump. To make a desired impression, you must overlive the cause you hope to make impressive."

When I asked for explanations of this kind of doubletalk, the Princes referred me to instances out of my own experience. It was true: to get something off the top shelf it was not enough to be able just to reach the shelf; I had to reach beyond it in order to get what I was after. When I found myself confronted by a rushing stream six-feet-wide, I had to jump at least seven feet in order to play safe. When I once saw Dr. Schweitzer gently brush some ants from a table and release them unharmed in the yard, he was *overliving* the concept of non-violence in order to impress on the world his contention that we should not kill unnecessarily and that we should not be wanton in our wholesale slaughter of human life.

There is something to be said for the overreach principle, but how do you overreach Broadway? Especially when you have the illusion that there is nothing better, not even an off-Broadway or a West Coast show.

The Princes explained it this way: They said that if I wanted to get a play on Broadway, I should not write with Broadway in mind. I should write with my own integrity in mind, and overreach into my wish and will for creative expression. My obsession about Broadway, they insisted, had put a check on me rather than a challenge. Whenever I sat down to write, the ghost of Broadway haunted me and either froze or mechanized my moods. I was trying to please Broadway rather than my own creative spirit. According to the Princes of Serendip, my aim and intentions were at fault. I should not have written so that I would get to Broadway, I should have written so that Broadway would get to me. A daring thought and comparable, I suppose, to the concept of the better mousetrap.

A goal that fills you with urgency or desperation can become a fixation, said the Princes. Overreach it. Make believe you have already reached it and you will relax and outdo yourself.

Reemphasizing the ancient truth that what we want too desperately eludes us constantly, the Princes tried to change my perspective and calm me down. Think how many a woman is still single, they suggested, or is single again, because she frantically wanted a man. Think how many of my plays are languishing in yellowing files because all I wanted was Broadway.

The Princes were generous with their axiomatic counsel:

"If you blow too hard into the fire, the smoke gets in your eyes."

"Hold a bird too tightly and you kill its song."

"Every overly ambitious man is a captive of his ambitions."

"If you cannot have what you want, want what you have, and soon you will have what you want."

"Better to bend to your fortune than to break under it."

"Patience can coax a hot spark from a cold stone."

"Pray that you never get all that you pray for."

And they always came back to the heart and core of serendipity: "The goals you find on the way to the goal you want may be more precious than the goal you seek."

I got to thinking about this during my "never on Broadway" lament, and I thought about it in the life experiences of people I know.

There was, for example, my friend Newt Weller. Newt

constantly had his heart set on discovering a method by which tornadoes could be detected and through which people could be effectively warned. An automotive expert, Newt could have had a comfortable, profitable life simply by following his profession. But as far back as twenty years ago when I first met him, he had this bug about tornadoes. An eccentric genius whose hometown accomplishments did not satisfy him, he took off to parts unknown. Figuratively speaking, he wanted "Broadway."

Through the years I kept up a Christmas-card correspondence with Newt and occasionally our paths crossed. He invented various items: automatic burglar alarms, mechanized signals for rural mail boxes, plastic gadgets of various kinds, all sorts of intriguing ideas materialized through his fertile mind. But whenever I saw him he was restless, successless, homeless, and getting little thrill out of his achievements because his eye was on "Broadway," the irresistible goal: a breakthrough in tornado warnings.

Then the other day I received a copy of a Midwest newspaper, the Des Moines *Register*, and on the front page was a headline; LAUD WELLER TORNADO WARNING SYSTEM. The story that followed was fascinating, and the information could conceivably save your life and mine.

Here is what happened. For years on end, Newt Weller had trudged the tornado trail. From land, sea, and air (he is a licensed flyer) he scanned the heavens. From a cluttered home laboratory to the sophisticated interior of the observatory, he pursued his quest. One day during a storm he turned on his television set. He noticed, as millions of viewers had done before him, that lightning flashes show up on the television screen in bright horizontal flashes. Then he turned down the brightness on the set to a point where there was a mere glimmer of light on the screen. Suddenly the screen was flooded with a total brightness. Shortly thereafter the terrifying whir of the wind and the roar of ominous sounds could be heard outside. Newt rushed out and there in the sky was the telltale cloud of a tornado.

Was it possible that his ordinary television set had served as a warning instrument? Was the flash of white light on the screen the signal he had been looking for, seeking everywhere except within his living room? Was it conceivable that he alone among the myriads of television viewers had made a breakthrough discovery?

Newt came up with a theory. A tornado funnel is in effect a giant, king-size vacuum tube and its effect on a television set works through an electronic linkage with the set when the adjustment has been made as follows: 1. Turn the brightness knob until screen is almost dark. 2. Watch to see when and if the entire screen lights up. 3. When the screen does light up and grows bright a tornado is on the way. Seek shelter!

Within days of the announcement, the Weller system became an Iowa household word. It was tornado season and throughout the state people began testing Newt's theory. Would it work? How far away could a tornado be detected? Would the warning allow sufficient time for the viewer to find safety?

At Orange City, Iowa, a family set the dials as directed during a lightning storm. Shortly thereafter the darkened screen blazed lightly. The viewers scurried to a basement shelter and the tornado came roaring in. Friends, who were visiting at the home, learned later that their own home ten miles away had been demolished.

The Weller system detected the big tornado that hit Belmond, Iowa. It caught the coming of a tornado that pounded Sheldon, Iowa. It reached out more than sixty miles to detect the tornado strikes that hit Charles City and Oelwein.

Paul Waite, climatologist for the U.S. Weather Bureau in Des Moines, praised the Weller method as the most significant discovery in the history of tornado research. "This," he said, "could be the answer to the government's search for a universal tornado warning system."

How does Newt feel about it? He is still not satisfied. Although everybody is talking about him and his discovery and despite the fact that it has been suggested that he be given a presidential citation, he feels he is not yet "on Broadway." What he wants is to discover a device that can be attached to television sets to automatically sound a tornado alarm. In fact, his goal is an instrumentation that will ingeniously permit lightning flashes to turn on the set and regulate the knobs!

I started to write Newt a letter congratulating him on his discovery and complimenting him on his tenacity and skill, but, thinking better of it, I decided first to send a mental communication to another source.

Dear Princes of Serendip:

Some time when you have a moment, clear up some questions for me.

1. Why is it that we are never quite content with our accomplishments? How come we have this eternal unrest? You have told us in no uncertain terms that our fringe goals are as important as our target goal, but somehow our minds don't work that way. Why?

2. Does anyone ever write to thank you for the counsel you have given us? It seems you have hit on a great secret when you tell us to count our blessings and when you suggest that the search is as thrilling as the discovery. Has anyone ever taken time to say, *"Merci beaucoup"*?

3. Is it possible that our eternal unrest is, after all, the quality that makes us westerners so inventive, progressive, and explorative? Even if we reached the ultimate goal (if there is such a thing), would we be satisfied?

Before I could finish the letter I had a call from a Little Theatre group in Houston, Texas. They wanted to do a play of mine in their next season's repertory. Would I be willing to have them do the production? "Yes," I said, "that would be fine with me."

As I put down the receiver I sat there thinking. Chicago, Denver, Hollywood, Philadelphia, Houston. Think of all the people who had seen my plays. I had so much to be grateful for.

Yet, as I thought it, an impish something deep within me, dim and distant as the din of a tornado, whispered, "But never on Broadway!"

But this time I had an answer: "You just wait!"

10

"CHANCE DAY"

*E*urope. Economy Class. For all the glamorous advertising of what is supposed to be fun, adventure, and pleasure in the friendly skies where the proud birds spread their silver wings, I can think of a dozen ways in which to spend eight hours more enjoyably. *First Class,* for example.

But my wife was quite right, as she had been on other flying occasions. She said, "I would rather go Economy Class than First Class and spend the money we save for things we want to buy. Furthermore, who wants to pay hundreds of dollars extra just for drinks and a little more leg room? Don't they advertise 'comfort and convenience' in Economy Class and don't the stewardesses always say, 'If there is anything we can do to make your flight more enjoyable, don't hesitate to call on us'?"

That is exactly what they said, in three different languages. But I have flown enough to know that there is nothing the stewardesses can do or will do to provide more space, not even on Swissair, unless they could bring in a crew of mechanics and take out half the seats.

Not a chance. The DC-8s that fly the sky between America and Europe have 124 economy spaces calibrated into two congested rows of three seats each on either side of a 22-inch aisle, so close together that only sardines would feel at home. The engineers who designed these interiors worked not in inches but in centimeters. The request to fasten your seat belt is unnecessary because you could not possibly be ejected once you are in, and when the table is down and your snack is served, you eat with a wrist motion only, for it is impossible to move your arm without knocking the hard roll off your neighbor's tray.

Nonetheless, when a person is economy-minded, he should make the best of it—which we did. My wife had a seat near the window, her feet squeezed in between her camera cases. I sat next to her with my long legs twisted into pretzels against a briefcase and a portable typewriter. Hopefully we held our breath in the expectation that the seat next to me would remain unoccupied, but the prospects were dubious. Everybody seemed bent on going to Zurich on this particular early evening flight.

Passengers came in all shapes and sizes—young servicemen, young mothers with children, girls in miniskirts and kookie glasses, elderly couples—tall, short lean, bulgy. As the moments passed and the line of passengers narrowed, I was about ready to move my legs when a middle-aged woman eyed the vacant seat and confirmed it to be her own. She was fat. Even when she removed her coat and asked me to hold it while she lengthened the seat belt to fit her contour, she was fat. A fat, motherly, roundfaced, red-cheeked, bespectacled *hausfrau* had come to ride with us—or we with her—to Switzerland.

It was not until we were five hours in flight and after we had gone through the calisthenics of supper that we engaged in some verbal give-and-take. I am sure the woman was as concerned about the discomfiture her bulges caused me as I was at the annoyance my squirming legs caused her, and as night came on we all had to get more chummy because of the need for walking up the aisle. Then we went through the acrobatics of getting back into our pressure chambers, to be reminded of what it used to be like to spend a night in a day coach.

Sleepless hours later the sight of the golden sun rising dramatically over the British Isles, the tray of rolls and coffee, and the prospect of being within reaching distance of our destination made us feel we could relax mentally, if not physically. So I started talking to the woman and learned that she was an American who lived in Zurich, where her husband was in the export-import business. The subject got around to my work and research, and I ventured to tell her that I was particularly interested in visiting a spiritualistic group which, I had been told, had its main base in Zurich but whose address I did not have with me. In response to this she drew me out some more on my interest in all this and then, as if having satisfied herself on my integrity in the matter, she remarked, "Well, you know, I happen to attend this group you are inquiring about. I think I can help you."

I sat in silent amazement. My wife nudged me as if to say, "Serendipity!" while I thought the same thing and tried again, as I so often have, to grasp the uncanny coincidences of life and the far-flung averages of chance.

Suddenly the Zurich airport was all too close and the time for me to absorb the information from my seat-mate was all too short. The woman had answers which saved me a great deal of time and tracking down of facts, all because I had gone Economy Class, and this one particular traveler had been guided to the seat adjoining mine. How could I ever again doubt the amazing world of serendipity?

Very likely I would doubt it, but hours later when I walked into the office of the Spiritualistic Society, I realized again that there is more to life than meets the eye and that the universe of which we are a part includes the unlimited mind of God as well as the limited mind of man.

Most of all, during my days in Zurich, I often thought of the many people I meet by chance who fit into the pattern of my life and work. Even more, I reflected on those individuals who unexpectedly influenced and improved the direction of my particular destiny. Have you ever thought about this? In fact, if you were asked to think of one person in particular who happened to cross your path and worked a certain magic on you, who would it be? Furthermore, have you ever told this person how much the meeting meant to you? Has anyone ever said to you, "You know, that chance encounter we had must have been more than mere chance?"

I had a sudden serendipitous inspiration. I decided that if I should ever be elected to Congress or if I ever met the head of a greeting card corporation, I would suggest the idea of a special "Chance Day" observance at which time we would pay tribute to chance acquaintances, chance friends, chance strangers, and drop them a note of appreciation.

I recognize, of course, that we are already overburdened with special days. I realize that every month of the year, with the exception of one, has more than its full share of holidays, holy days, or special days for which we buy more than three billion dollars' worth of greeting cards and pay another billion-plus in postage. You can make your own list from January's New Year's Day through June's Graduation Days to December's Christmas Day, and you will find that the only month that is actually cardless is August.

This, in the light of serendipity, is tremendously significant for, according to legend, it was in August (August 7, to be exact) that the Princes of Serendip rested in their travels and observed "Chance Day" with special observances. They dispatched letters of appreciation to those whom chance had steered their way and who had given their life a lift or filled their days with special light and love. After my experience on the plane I felt that the world needed a day like this even if it meant another greeting card or the writing of a special note.

> Thanks to chance
> You came my way!
> Three cheers for Serendipity!

I thought of a dozen people without half trying, people who came out of nowhere, called by a guidance higher than mine, directed by a power greater than my own, and motivated by a wisdom more knowledgeable than any I possessed—people indispensable in the total meaning of my life. And as I thought about them I wondered if there might be individuals out there in the whirling world who felt the same way about remembering me. In fact, it gave me a sense of worthwhileness to think there might be one or two who would send me a note on "Chance Day." Such a wish, of course, was somewhat contrary to the Princes of Serendip because they rarely thought of themselves as being on the receiving end of things.

"Chance Day."

I am thinking not of friends or relatives or acquaintances with whom we logically have fellowship, but of people we meet Economy Class or First Class (or any class, for that matter) in serendipitous encounters. For example, one day I had a letter from a woman (whom I will call H. J. B.) who had received one of my books from another woman, who just happened to have the book lying on her desk. Here was no prompting, planning, or plotting of any kind. It was all pure chance. Then H. J. B. wrote me asking whether I would autograph copies of several of my books for friends of hers who lived in foreign countries. This started a chain reaction that has put me in touch with people all around the world.

Or consider the fact that one day I was held up in a Midwestern hotel by a blizzard, and it was because of this that I met a man who was instrumental in effecting a teaching appointment for me, which gave my life an entirely new direction. Or how about the time a story of mine appeared in Unity's *Good Business* under the title, "Ponies Are Part of God's Kingdom"? This piece was reprinted in a professional horsemen's magazine and through it I met Perry Holmes of Birmingham, Michigan, who has figured in my life. If the truth were told, my life from meeting the girl I married to following the career in which I am now engaged has been the result of unexpected happenings, enough to convince me that I am in debt to a higher guidance and that I should set aside a "Chance Day" to remind myself and others of the fact.

Whenever I read biographies it becomes clear to me that though chance may seem unique, it is also universal. Mark Twain was influenced by a chance meeting with Henry Ward Beecher. George Bernard Shaw did not really find himself until he happened to drop in on a lecture given by

Henry George. Mahatma Gandhi was given direction for his life when he accidentally met a group of Tolstoyians. William Penn chanced to hear a Quaker named Lee, and a new state was founded in America. Thomas Alva Edison, a grammar school drop-out, was fascinated by American inventors and went on to be admitted to the National Academy of Science, having added to the world's light and music.

Think of the universality of chance next time you read about famous personalities, or when next you open your Bible. There is no greater serendipitous book in the world than the Scriptures. Think of the debt Noah owed to the Lord (and the Lord to Noah) when they met by chance to talk about the flood. Consider Abraham when he unexpectedly entertained angels, or Jacob when he wrestled with the mysterious stranger, or Saul, who met Samuel while looking for his father's asses. Reflect on the coincidence that the daughter of Pharoah came down to bathe where the child Moses lay in his ark in the bullrushes. Consider the parable of the Good Samaritan in which it is said, "Now by *chance* a priest was going down that road. . . ."

"Pious folk," says the Interpreter's Bible, "have always hailed chance as the personal pleasure ground of the God of Law, where He is free from official legality and can at times waive such principles as those of cause and effect and act with arbitrary kindliness and favor. However, God operates by laws we have not been able to analyze and at the utmost bounds of human effort when we have done all we can to attain the desired end."

Yes, "Chance Day" should by rights be made a legal holiday on August 7, a time for remembrance and gratitude to those who cross our path in the labyrinth of life, those who pass like ships in the night, or who, like angels unaware, come to bless and underwrite the way that we should go. "Chance Day," a day in which to remember that every good thing communicates itself to whoever is able to receive it—a day to pause with the Princes of Serendip and take note of the fact that in the tomorrows just ahead there will be new faces, new forms, new strangers who will become fellow-voyagers and friends.

Anything that makes us more interrelated with all life is good. To see ourselves as part of a universal plan, to sense an involvement, to catch on to an expanding openness with the world, to realize that there are dimensions beyond the commonly seen and experiences beyond the ordinarily felt, these are enriching qualities. Everything about life points to the fact that we are not alone, that our faith is not static or fixed, that our position in the nature of things is not limited by any sense of restriction. There *is* something beyond the commonplace. There *are* ways beyond our knowing. There *is* abiding proof that the unseen is as important and as instrumental in our destiny as are the forces we presume to govern and control.

Let's believe it, and know that we are in debt to strangers and in kinship with all life whose visions are part of a universal mind and heart.

Everyone in favor of "Chance Day" say "Aye!"

11
THE SECRET WHISPER

*A*mong the apocryphal stories of the Princes of Serendip (that is, those stories which may or may not be authentic) is the one about their "secret whisper."

It seems that when an individual would come to them with problems and matters of concern, the Princes would listen patiently, carefully weigh what they heard, and then they would quietly whisper a few words into their client's ear. This practice worked such miracles and had such phenomenal effect that it got to be a much sought-after therapy. Evidently the client was pledged not to divulge the secret whisper and this added to its effectiveness.

Gradually, however, as the Princes moved on into new

territory along the serendipity road, the mystery was cleared up. Every once in a while someone would divulge the Princes' advice by passing the magic words along to someone who needed help. That recipient would immediately find himself involved in his own great adventure. Soon it became known that the secret whisper consisted of two simple words: *"Surprise yourself!"*

I discovered the effectiveness of these words in a most wonderful way. In fact, you might say it was a case of serendipity itself.

I was in the mountains of British Columbia carrying a camper's pack on my back and I was very tired. It was getting late, and for me to go back over the trail I had come was a long, tedious walk. There was a shortcut, however, which would more than cut the distance in half, but to take this route meant that I would have to walk across a twenty-foot log which spanned a ravine. The ravine fell away from a sheer precipice some thirty feet deep, and the log that served as a bridge was a mere eight or ten inches in diameter. This was a precarious passage.

Everyone in that part of the country knew about the shortcut and many people thought nothing about crossing this narrow span. Even kids had used it, and once I saw a dog run across it as if it were as safe as the George Washington Bridge. But I was not given to "high places." My sense of balance had never qualified me as a tightrope artist by any means. I was reminded of this now as I walked to the edge of the ravine and gingerly looked down. It was steep, deep, and dangerous.

I sat down on a rock, musing about the log and me.

Some hopefully helpful sayings came to mind. I remembered that someone, somewhere, once said, "Do the thing you fear!" That sounded valiant, all right, but had the speaker ever walked the "narrow bridge"?

Another thought came to me: "It's all in your mind." That was a handy phrase, too, but just now I felt it was all in my equilibrium. After all, some people have a sense of balance and some haven't. Well, I did have *sort* of a sense of balance, I told myself, remembering how, as a boy, I had walked railroad tracks and done fairly well.

This brought me around to the example I had run across in a number of books on the power of the mind and the impressiveness of the unconscious. You can walk a narrow plank on the ground without any qualms. Raise the plank several inches and you will still feel confident. But raise it still higher, suspend it between two walls with a drop-off below, and what happens? At what point do you "get scared"? When and why do you suddenly "lose your sense of balance"? At what height are you daunted by the fear of falling?

These thoughts played games in my mind as I eyed the passive log. It was tightly wedged between the rocks; it could not roll or become dislodged. It was a sturdy bridge, all right, but just now it looked as narrow as a razor's edge.

Then the Princes of Serendip flashed into mind. There they were, asking me to bow my ear while they gave me the secret whisper, "*Surprise yourself!*"

Now I am not suggesting this to anyone less inclined to the impossible than I, and I am not saying that someone with a chronic case of vertigo should follow my lead. I am simply reporting that something deep in my subjective mind began to stir and throb and lift me to my feet until I was within stepping distance of the log.

I adjusted my pack. I tested my walking shoes to see whether or not they were inclined to slip. I stepped poised and proud to the edge of the log. "*Surprise yourself!*"

What a great feeling! What a self-satisfying, masterly thrill to take a forward step and leave your fears behind, or to put them into the pack on your back and say, "I can carry you, too, in case you're wondering!" What a marvelous experience to "surprise yourself!"

I will not say it was a perfectly executed crossing, but it was a courageous one, and a super-self within me proved to the hesitant me that it could be done. I have had a more balanced, less shaky feeling ever since.

Just how all this works remains something of a mystery. In a way, the conscious mind persuades the subjective mind that it is willing to take the chance, and in return the subjective mind tells the conscious mind that it has nothing to fear and that *it can be done*. The giant persuader, however, is the "secret whisper."

Would I have done it if I hadn't known I could do it? Probably not. Evidently the level of action is raised when we take an affirmative position and decide to meet a situation head-on. I visualized the log as being on the ground, not thirty feet above the yawning gap. It was not a state of distance but a state of mind that turned the trick—and today, while my common sense tells me not to be overly foolhardy, I enjoy the lure of walking where I would have hesitated before I dared to walk the narrow bridge.

Sometimes I get to wondering about the unlimited capabilities of professionals in any field, be they performers on the tightwire or those who meet the day-by-day problems of life with equally special expertise. Who can measure the power of the secret whisper when a Prince of Serendip asks you to bend an ear?

Take, for example, the agonizing fight some people carry on with the smoking habit or the eating habit or the drinking habit. They try pills and cures and therapies galore. They discuss their problems with their friends and their analysts. They go the round of behavorial sessions, and I have run into them in dozens of retreats where they are trying to find some rub-off magic as the answer to their need. I wonder what would happen if they took matters into their own hands with their own inner resources and listened to a voice within saying, "*Surprise yourself!*"

I will always remember a friend of mine who whipped a special weakness by coming around full circle to this conclusion: "I got myself into this mess and therefore I can get myself out of it."

If you are in the habit of surprising yourself with fear, you can rest assured that you have the ability also to surprise yourself with courage and faith. If you are sure you are weak, you can be doubly sure you are strong. The quickness of the process of self-discovery depends on the intensity of your will to surprise yourself, for obviously it is the "deeper you" that does the surprising. Somewhere I once read, "Any inadequacy felt in the hope of attaining something you truly want is the forerunner of the attainment."

With me it was walking a twenty-foot log, ten inches wide. With others it is other things. To strengthen the weakest link in life, the secret seems to be the secret whisper, for it is obvious that those who close their ears to the Princes' suggestion not only leave a great deal of unfinished business, but stand in danger of losing a great deal of the joy of life.

This was impressed on my by a talk I had with a small-town banker. He told me that every year someone among his clientele dies intestate, leaving a strongbox full of money, without instructions for its disposition. He told me of one case where a recluse, fearful of banks, buried his cold cash in cans on various parts of his property. Across the country, billions of dollars are hoarded and hidden by people who live as though they were paupers. Then they die and there is either a wild scramble for their fortune or else the money lies unknown and unclaimed, gathering dust, awaiting the due process of the law.

The banker told me about a woman in a nearby city who went out every day scavenging through refuse barrels and dumpyards picking up discarded bottles—pop bottles, beer bottles, vinegar bottles, all kinds of bottles. She would take these to a secondhand dealer and barter with him in order to get a few pennies to feed her emaciated body.

One day this woman failed to show up and it was discovered that she had died, largely of self-neglect. In her stuffy single-room apartment, in the midst of meager surroundings, authorities found $70,000 in cash in a dresser drawer, and a savings book showing that the woman had $80,000 on deposit, money she had inherited when she was a girl.

It occurred to the banker that patterns set early in life become more fixed and rigid as time goes on. Apparently there are times when no one comes along to effect a change in thinking. Apparently, too, no one has yet found the magic key that can unlock the layaway treasures in safe-deposit vaults, or release the obvious reminder that "you can't take it with you."

It occurred to me that this happens not only with money and securities but also with things of the heart and mind. We hoard and hide our good intentions. We become niggardly with our affections. We stash away our friendly impulses under lock and key, or bury them in cans around our premises. Isn't it just as ridiculous to leave a lot of unfinished goodness after one's demise as it is to leave a lot of money that has never been used and is undesignated for any constructive good?

The Princes of Serendip had a way of getting us over all this. They had the secret whisper: "Do the unexpected. *Surprise yourself!*"

12
WHY DID
WHAT HAPPENED, HAPPEN?

While doing some work in the Los Angeles Public Library the other day, I was startled by the soft sound of someone calling my name. I looked up. A young man in his mid-twenties apologized for having intruded into my reading. "I thought it was you but I wasn't sure," he said. "I want to shake your hand and thank you for something you did for me three years ago."

"Good," I said. "That helps my day."

"Three years ago," he explained, "you spoke in Carnegie Hall in New York, for the Unity people. I attended the meeting. At the time I was trying to decide where to invest my life. Something you said that morning helped me make my decision. I decided then and there to go into the ministry."

He gave me his name——Gene Holden——and informed me he was now pastor of a Negro church in Los Angeles (The Tabernacle), where he and his people are carrying on an interesting and integrated work.

I am always meeting people unexpectedly. Very likely you are, too. Have you learned, as I have, to be more courteous to strangers (they might be friends)? As, for example, the morning I was making a telephone call between planes at the St. Louis airport. There, protruding from an adjoining booth, were a man's legs practically barring my door. I thought to myself, "What nerve!" But when my gaze followed the legs to their rightful owner I discovered it was a former student of mine, Dr. Ken Berg, who once told me he admired me for my even temper. You never know.

There was the day in traffic when a car suddenly pulled up in front of me and I was ready to give the driver a piece of my mind. When our eyes met we recognized each other and smiled and drove to a nearby coffee shop. He was a play producer who was interested in one of my scripts.

One of the best of these serendipitous encounters happened recently when my wife and I were in northern California. She wanted to get pictures of Mt. Shasta at the psychological moment when the sun's rays were dramatically touching the snow-crowned summit. We pulled into an isolated area, positive we would be undisturbed in setting up the tripod and all the other details. We had just gotten nicely started when an Airstream trailer pulled up next to our car. The driver immediately engaged us in conversation about the weather, the beauty of Shasta, the camera angles, and so on. Politeness prevented me from expressing my true feelings, and evidently he didn't get my unspoken message. He kept on talking. Then a woman stepped from the trailer and, lo, it was a friend of ours who had recently married the gentleman at the wheel. We had a great visit together and incidently got some excellent shots of the mountain.

I never cease to marvel at the infinite timing involved in these seeming coincidences. I never get over the synchronized, split-second planning that some mysterious guidance behind the scenes exercises to bring about the unexpected. At such times I think of the Princes of Serendip. They accepted these circumstances as thrilling scenes in the play of life, and often at evening time they enjoyed discussing among themselves the tantalizing question, "Why did what happened, happen?"

They had three answers to this question, and each added charm and a new dimension to their involvement in passing events. The first answer was this: *"What happened, happened either for your growth or for your guidance."*

Obviously the way to test the validity of this first point is to sit back and reflect on the effect that inexplicable circumstances have had on *your* life. Think about it for a moment. How many coincidental meetings with unexpected people in unlooked-for places proved to be turning points in your life or your career? If you made a list of things that happened to you without your knowing at the time *why* they happened, how many would you *now* say resulted in growth or guidance for you?

Yes, we should by rights use our own experiences as touchstones, but the history of others is also fascinating and instructive. I have just been reading a biography of one of the loneliest men who ever lived, the philosopher Arthur Schopenhauer (1788-1860). Truth is, he is known as the "pessimistic philosopher," and is supposed to have said, "Were I a king, my prime command would be, 'Leave me alone!' " When Arthur was a boy, his father died by drowning and his mother, an advocate of free love, went a-wandering. Schopenhauer, virtually an orphan, grew to young manhood groping for an understanding of life. Proud of his intellectual capabilities, offending people by his egotistical claims (masks to hide his loneliness), he was aloof, friendless, and literally and figuratively always walked alone except for the companionship of his poodle. Once when he thought he was alone he bent over a rose and began speaking lovingly to the flower. A gardener came by at this serendipitous moment, watched and listened, and said in all earnestness, "Who are you?" Schopenhauer replied, "Ah, if you could tell me *that,* you would be the greatest philosopher in all the world."

Having said this he realized that if *he* could answer the question, "Who am I?" he would also be the greatest of all philosophers. How could he discover himself and realize his potentials?

One day after his mother had settled down, he visited her. She was having a party. A group of children, catching sight of Schopenhauer's serious, brooding face, laughed at him. He *was* a strange figure, a kind of eighteenth-century hippie with heavy sideburns and bushy tufts of hair that stood out above his ears. Hurt by the attitude of the children, he walked mournfully away and stood at a window gazing out despondently. The taunts of the young people were suddenly cut short by a deep German voice, "Children, don't laugh at that young man. In time he will surpass us all."

Schopenhauer turned and met the thoughtful gaze of the speaker, a man named Goethe, proclaimed as the greatest genius of the eighteenth century. The words rang through Schopenhauer's mind: "He will surpass us all." It had been a chance encounter, but the philosopher-pessimist never forgot it. All his life he had hoped to meet someone who would turn the key in his creative mind and help him find himself. He found himself now. Though he never let it be known, Goethe became his inspiration and idol. He still walked alone with his dog but, it was said, never without the spiritual presence of Goethe. After a long-awaited but ultimate recognition, when he had finally achieved victory in life, Schopenhauer chose to die seated in a chair beneath the picture of the German poet.

Why did what happened, happen at the party in his mother's home? It *was* either for guidance or for growth. Or both.

The Princes of Serendip had another explanation for the coincidental moment. Why did what happened, happen? They said, *"Because you drew the happening to yourself by conscious or unconscious forces within yourself."*

Have you heard of *I Ching?* It is a book, one of the five classics of Confucianism and, if your imagination can grasp it, goes back to the twelfth century *B.C.* and is, no doubt, one of the oldest treatises in the world. *I Ching* means *"Book of Changes."* A new translation has just appeared by Wilhelm Baynes (Princeton Press) and the more than 700 pages may leave you thoroughly overwhelmed, as they did me. But the gist of *I Ching* is this: By tossing coins or counting marrow sticks in keeping with a prescribed computation, a key or equation is provided with which you can consult the *I Ching* and get a hint of what is going on in your unconscious mind, a revelation of the days ahead, or a suggestion to a solution of a problem.

Dr. C. G. Jung, in a foreword to a previous edition of *The Book of Changes,* made some interesting observations. "The moment under actual observation," said Jung, "appears to the ancient Chinese view more of a chance hit than a clearly defined result of concurring causal chain processes. The matter of interest seems to be the configuration formed by chance events in the moment of observation, and not at all the hypothetical reasons that seemingly account for the coincidence. While the Western mind carefully sifts, weighs, selects, classifies, and isolates, the Chinese concept of the moment encompasses everything down to the minutest nonsensical detail, because all of the ingredients make up the observed moment."

Jung was unusually qualified to interpret the aspects of *I Ching* because he once coined a word, *synchronicity,* which suggested that the coincidence of events in space and time meant something more than mere chance, namely, "a peculiar interdependence of objective events among themselves as well as with the subjective states of the observer." This means, in effect, that every moment of life is a convergence point in which our psychic state, our thoughts, our frame of mind, and so on, are interrelated with the frame of reference in our environment. This is where conscious and unconscious forces come in. The way we think, feel, act, imagine, wish, or suppose ourselves to be, all converge to cause us to *be* a certain way, and we attract happenings by these forces within ourselves. Yet there is also something in our surroundings which interplays on these emotions and thoughts and we, in turn, influence them, our surroundings.

So when we toss a handful of coins in the air and they fall in a certain pattern with a certain number of heads and tails, this is exactly the way they were supposed to fall at that moment; if we had a key or a clue as to *why* they fell this way, then we would also have a hint of the state of our being when they fell this way. The *I Ching* claims to offer such a revelation. Obviously it is still a speculative science for, at best, we cannot do away with the element of chance *in* chance, and still have chance left over! In this respect chance is somewhat comparable to faith, for if we could always be sure absolutely we would not need faith—but unless we have faith, we will never be absolutely sure.

Here, again, the best test would be to sit down at evening time, as the Princes did, and ask yourself what happened to you during the day and how much of what happened, happened because you *drew* the happening to yourself. This attitudinizing or fantasizing is inherent in the concept of spiritual thinking, all the way from the simple matter of starting a new day to embarking on a lunar flight. Your own personality, your own psyche, your own attitude, all are involved in the outcome of the events that happen to you, and you will realize this when evening comes and you sit down and think it over. (The trick, of course, is to realize all of this in the morning *before you begin your day*.)

In connection with I Ching the word aleatory has come into vogue. Coming from the Latin, *alea,* which means a dice game, *aleatory* has long been a legal term used in references to the element of chance. But now there is such a thing as *aleatory* art. You put colors in the muzzle of an air gun, aim it at a canvas, and shoot, letting the spray fall where it may. There are now aleatory drawings. Close your eyes and let the pencil in your hand trace its unconscious design, come what will.

A contemporary composer, John Cage, flips coins and uses the *I Ching* to construct aleatory musical compositions. A photographer, Alvin Wheeler, shoots his camera from the hip and develops his aleatory photographs.

At a Unity retreat in Pawling, New York, I sat in on a class where we practiced aleatory sculpture using molding wax. We held the pliable wax in our hands, put our minds at rest, then let our hands fashion and shape the responsive wax into whatever our subconscious mind dictated. This was done in reverent silence and at the end of twenty minutes when we opened our eyes, we realized that even the least artistic among us had come up with interesting and often astonishing aleatory masterpieces. The Princes of Serendip would have said, "You are expressing the happening by conscious or unconscious forces within yourself."

Why did what happened, happen? The Princes had a third explanation, *"What happened, happened not for your benefit, but for the benefit and profit of someone else."*

This is truly a most insightful thought and if we can grasp it, it will help us immeasurably in our adjustment to total life. For how often do you catch yourself saying, "Why did this person come to *me?* Why did I have to meet *him* or *her?* What made *this* character cross my path?" One thing is certain up to now: when anything happened to us we have been inclined to think only in terms of what it meant to *us.* The possibility that we were conceivably a catalyst, an influence, or a factor in the life of someone else rarely entered our mind. Now that we have been introduced to the world of serendipity, chance happenings take on a transpersonal relationship. No longer do we live "to ourselves alone"; we take others into account and, as the Princes often said, "When chance becomes a pleasure, life becomes a play."

In the apocryphal stories of preachers is one about the minister in a Massachusetts town who went to his tiny Unitarian church one stormy night. His audience that night consisted of just one young man. No one else had braved the storm. The minister said to himself, "Why did this happen to *me?* Why did this fellow have to come and why must I preach just to *him?*" But he did. He preached to his audience of one, but that one, so the story goes, was Dwight L. Moody, who became one of America's greatest evangelists (so great, in fact, that it was said of him that he robbed hell of a hundred thousand souls). And the minister who preached on that raw and callous night eventually realized that what happened had happened not for him, but for the benefit of Brother Moody.

This third point was also the theme of a purportedly true story told by Aulus Gellius. He reported that a slave who ran away from a cruel taskmaster in Africa took refuge in a cave. Hiding in the half-dark of the dank surroundings, the slave was thanking his lucky stars for his escape when a shadow appeared in the cave's entrance. At first he thought it was his master, then he realized it was something conceivably worse: a lion. We can imagine what went through the poor slave's mind, "Why did this happen to *me!*"

The lion crouched. Then it crawled slowly into the cave. The hapless slave retreated until he stood with his back against the wall. The lion paused and held up his right paw. It was bruised and bleeding. In it was a thorn. The slave, whose name by the way was Androcles, gathered up his courage and extracted the thorn with the greatest of care, and the lion gratefully licked his helper's hand and departed.

Three years later in Rome, Androcles, who had become a Christian, was seized by Roman persecutors and ordered to renounce his faith. He refused and was sentenced to fight a lion in the Roman arena. This, of course, meant sudden death, but for the fact that the lion, which had been brought from the African wilds, was the same one Androcles had befriended. This king of the jungle recognized his benefactor and, instead of attacking him, showered him with such affection that Androcles was granted his freedom. He was even hailed as a miracle worker by those who believed he had some supernatural power (which, of course, he did have: the supernatural power of chance.) George Bernard Shaw wrote a play about this— *Androcles and the Lion.* People saw a lesson in it. And as you think about it now a montage of similar stories may come to mind, including lions you may have befriended and thorns you have plucked from swollen paws, and perhaps someday if you are ever thrown into the arena, all will be well with you too.

At any rate, when you have a chance to sit down at evening time and think back over your day or days, when you wistfully shake your head and wonder, "Why did what happened, happen?" remember the Princes of Serendip. They had three answers: 1. It happened either for your growth or for your guidance. 2. It happened because you drew what happened to yourself by conscious or unconscious forces. 3. It happened not for your benefit but for the benefit of someone else—and that someone else, of course, may have been you.

13

THE FATE MAKERS

I used to envy them. They got the breaks, I had to struggle for mine. They were on top of things, I let things get me down. I felt at the mercy of chance, they governed it. Then I got to know them and gradually learned that there were reasons why good fortune favored them. There is a great deal more behind their lives than meets the eye. I call them "the fate makers."

A case in point was Tony Garzell who won a hundred-yard dash against a field of six challengers. After he victoriously crossed the finish line and someone asked him why he had been so confident, Tony said, "Why shouldn't I run the hundred yards? After all, I'm a hundred and one!" That's right: Tony Garzell was a hundred and one years of age. His opponents were in their late sixties. He outran them, outthought them, outlaughed them in good humor after the race was run. Tony the fate maker.

To look at Tony you would think he was just like any other man about town. There were a few things he didn't do. He didn't smoke and he didn't drink and to hear him tell it he had old-fashioned ideas about sex; and if you saw Tony working at his job as doorman at the Delano Hotel or if you followed him in a day's routine, you wouldn't see much in Tony's life that was different from that of any other half-way decent individual. "Oh, well," you say, "he must have come from good stock. His mother probably lived to be 110 and his father 120 and, as the saying goes, he was smart in choosing his ancestors." Not so with Tony. His parents died in their early seventies.

Well, then, he had a good fate. That was true. He had a good fate. But the truth of the matter was, he helped make it. There were habits Tony had and things Tony did when no one was watching that made Tony different from others and helped to make him what he was.

For one thing, he had a love for life. He liked to laugh and he loved to listen. He was such a good listener that often when his information was better than the information someone gave him, he just said, "Yes, sir. Yes, *sir*. Well, now, you don't say!" He told me that this approach added years to his life, and maybe it did.

For another thing, he was grateful. He was grateful for health, a job, friends, memories, and the hope for tomorrow. Most of all, without trying to fantasize about the man, I think his greatest gratitude was for little things: the weather whatever it was, people whoever they were, another day however it went.

He rarely talked about his age, and the publicity he got

about the hundred-yard dash would not have happened if it had been left up to him. He was neither old nor young, to hear him tell it, he just *was*. As for taking care of himself, medical check-ups, vitamins and all that sort of thing, he was strictly neutral. He had his own secrets, obvious ones, old ones: long, quiet walks, simple exercises, regular habits, restful sleep (once a month he slept around the clock), no special health fads, and a few axioms. "Food must be chewed." "Relax to eat, eat to relax." "What can't be cured must be endured, but believe that you can cure it." "Do unto others, but don't forget to do unto yourself."

Tony the fate maker. A lucky guy, but no luckier than I for having met him and for having looked behind the scenes in his life to see what makes a centenarian tick—for a hundred years and one.

People like Tony were those the Princes of Serendip must have had in mind when they said, "The most important person you can meet on the serendipity road is you!" Now think of that! Think how often you and I have wished to meet someone who could help us get that break or lift that load or turn that trick or score that point or get us over that hump! "Oh, for a fate maker!" we sighed.

"First of all," said the Princes of Serendip, "you must meet yourself."

Now that can be a startling encounter. It really can. I remember walking through an art gallery one day, a large and momentarily quite deserted place. At the far end of a hallway a man came toward me, a tall, slender man, rather confident, I thought, neatly dressed and carrying a topcoat over his arm just as I was carrying mine. And why not? With a sudden shock I realized that the man I saw was *me*, walking straight into myself by way of a floor-to-ceiling crystal mirror. Without too much narcissism, I trust, I stopped and looked this man over from top to toe as if for the first time. He looked normal, quite normal: two arms, two legs, a face, a form, a consciousness. A fate maker if only he would believe it! Thank you, Princes of Serendip, for the introduction!

Man, whenever he finds himself (thinking man, that is), has all the potentialities he needs to adjust himself to his world. The assignment is to recognize these potentials, to draw them out, *educare*, the ultimate aim of education. For many thinking men, what they thoughtlessly call the "real self" is in conflict with the ideal. Or maybe it is the other way around. No matter. Something there is within oneself that says, "All you need to truly live is here in you." When the thought gets hold of you it never lets you go, and the Princes of Serendip keep walking, saying not another word.

Here's a game you can play. Pick a name, any name, out of the hopper of history and take a new look at the man or woman you have picked. Try to see this person from behind the scenes, the make-up room, as it were, where he prepared himself to play his role in the show of life. See how he made his fate. Take anyone—rich man, poor man, beggarman, thief. If historic figures or contemporary personalities are too elusive, take someone you know or wish you knew. For example, take my Aunt Selma.

Perhaps you never heard of my Aunt Selma. Few people outside of the little Wisconsin village where she lived ever did. But as I look back on her now, I can see that she was a fate maker. For example, she used to be annoyed by all sorts of things: a wall switch that continually caused the living room lights to flicker, a door that squeaked, letters she misplaced, shoes that got scattered in the closet. She often lost her temper. She was single, my youngest aunt, and she wanted a man.

My mother, who was Selma's sister, said it was this longing for a man that made Aunt Selma fidgety. Be that as it may, one day for no apparent reason Selma turned to fate-making. Don't ask me why. It could have been an act of desperation, or self-assertion, or sudden awakening, or maybe she read something in the *Ladies' Home Journal*. At any rate, Aunt Selma went downtown and came back with a can of oil for the squeaky door, a letter file for her mail, a shoe rack for the closet, and an electrician to fix the switch. In one afternoon she cleared up these annoyances and then set about correcting others.

By the same mysterious transition, Aunt Selma began to dress up instead of dressing down. She was really quite pretty but she used to say, "When God gave out good looks, I wasn't around." Evidently she now thought she would begin to work with what God had given her and go on from there. Then one day she announced to our family that the electrician had asked her to marry him and she had accepted. He was a bachelor who was considered quite a catch around town. They got married and lived happily ever after, and my mother often wondered about those living room lights that flickered and the switch that had always needed fixing. Aunt Selma the fate maker.

I recently ran across a most unusual man in the fate-maker category. He is a minister and the envy of many in his profession, because he has undisputed authority in his church and a freedom that is second to none. No church board or bishop or district superintendent tells him what to do, and if ever there was a free spirit in the institutionalized world of faith it is the Reverend John H. Wells.

What's more, his church is one of the most popular in California, and certainly among the best known in Greater Los Angeles. People of all creeds, Christian and non-Christian alike, know and appreciate The Little Brown Church in the Valley and its dedicated and denominationally independent pastor. Officially he is affiliated with the Disciples of Christ, but even they accept him as something of a law unto himself. His church never locks its doors, collection plates are never passed, and you can summon the minister any time, day or night, simply by pressing a button inside the church's open doors.

For those clerics who occasionally wish couples would drop into their church or chapel to get married, The Little Brown Church in the Valley is the envy of the West Coast. The other day Pastor Wells had fifteen weddings, and he smilingly told me it was an average day. His counseling is an even greater service and people come to him continually for help and guidance. They see the sign on Coldwater Canyon which says, "Come in and pray." They slip into the quiet little church and feel its warmth. They meet the seemingly unhurried and outgoing minister and some are tempted to say, "He's lucky. He must have been born under a good star or had a pull with authorities higher up."

That may be true, if you go up high enough. For John H. Wells some thirty years ago decided to work with the Lord and cooperatively make his fate. In 1939 he acquired a piece of property in North Hollywood and started to build a church. I mean by hand, from the ground up, with hammer and nails and a vision and a prayer. People stopped by in those days and said, "What're you building?" "A church," Wells would say, and often the inquirer would reply, "Oh, yeah?" But when the structure began to take form, there were those who came with a will to work and to have a tiny share in building this house of the Lord, matching up the knotty pine, fashioning the belfry and adding their volunteer touches to the kneeling altar and the windows which open to the valley's friendly foliage and God's blue sky.

One day a youngster watched Wells at work.

"What are you going to call your church?" the boy asked wistfully.

"I don't know," Wells said. "What do you think I should call it?"

"Little Brown Church," said the boy.

"All right," the minister replied, "that's what I'll call it."

And he did. So a congregation grew and soon it became traditional to be married in the quiet, worshipful sanctuary or to turn for help or service to The Little Brown Church.

I found John Wells to be a combination of a rock-ribbed champion of the Lord Jesus Christ while maintaining an ecumenical spirit that reached into the questing heart of everyman. Theologically conservative and interculturally liberal, highly realistic but full of dreams, he is wise with years and young of heart. But most of all, I found him to be a fate maker.

And the Princes of Serendip kept walking in the vision of my mind, and I heard them say that when you truly meet yourself—whether it is in running the hundred-yard dash or walking in an art museum, getting someone to fix an eccentric switch, or building a little brown church in a valley—when you meet yourself, you have taken the first exciting step toward being a fate maker in the wonderful world of serendipity.

14

THE FEED-FORWARD
FORMULA

*U*nless you are a physician, a mathematician, a philosopher, or a finalist in a spell-down you may never have heard the word *apocatastasis*. Nor would I bother you with it were it not for the fact that it could conceivably solve many a problem for you, get you out of the doldrums or, if you should need it, restore your will to live.

Look at it again: *apocatastasis!*

There is evidence that the Princes of Serendip imparted both the word and its secret power to some of their initiates. At least a story illustrating the point has come down to us.

It seems that one day a man named Sabi Ben Suh came

to the Princes for consultation, while they were passing through the ancient region of Polonnaruwa in old Ceylon. Sabi Ben Suh, a young, handsomely accoutered *mirza* (man of nobility) disconsolately told the Princes his unfortunate story. A flood had washed away his newly-built summer home on a beautiful estate which he had purchased at great cost on the banks of a river. The irony about it was that the stream had never been known to flood, but no sooner had Sabi Ben Suh built his house than the waters came, leaving him poorer and no wiser. No wiser, that is, until one of the Princes looked at him observingly and said, "Apocatastasis!"

Three years later when the Princes of Serendip returned to Polonnaruwa a messenger came to them with an invitation from the *mirza*. Sabi Ben wanted them to visit him in his new summer mansion situated on a lovely promontory, high above the river. What had happened? Well, the devastation of his former home had forced him to search for new territory. He discovered not only the new location but a field of pure agates, which were priceless because of their use as talismen and amulets to guard the wearer from disaster.

"Oh, my Princes!" exclaimed Sabi Ben Suh. "But for your assurance of apocatastasis I would never have had the patience or the faith to have what is mine today. But for you I would have spent my days in remorse!"

The Princes smiled and said, "If only all men could learn the secret! If only everyone could remember the saying, 'Until tomorrow becomes today, men will be blind to the good fortune hidden in unfortunate acts.' "

The *mirza* bowed low and said, "How true it is. Until tomorrow becomes today, we are reluctant to believe."

What he was saying was that even when he stood in the devastation of his flood-wrecked home, the art of apocatastasis had helped him project his thoughts out of the ruins and into that distant day when good would come out of seeming misfortune.

Apocatastasis: *The serendipitous secret that in every seed of seeming tragedy is hidden the fruit of glory and reward.*

I call it "The Feed-Forward Formula," which is to say that in a moment of despair or seemingly irreversible circumstances we should send our thoughts on a shaft of faith into the tomorrow where the full meaning of today becomes apparent. Is this easy or simple? Not always. It requires courage, control, and audacious confidence, no less than humble obedience to the Unseen. It needs a touch of what romantic realists call *amor fati*, love of fate.

Try it for yourself next time you are in an indigo mood or when your dream house is washed away by a flash flood. Try it when the unexpected happens and you find yourself asking, "Why?" or "What next?" or "What possible good can come out of this?" Try the wonder-working power of the feed-forward formula, or apocatastasis.

To the physician it means that the wound will heal, the broken bone will mend, the pain will cease. To the mathematician apocatastasis is the infallible belief in eternal recurrence. To the philosopher it means reestablishment of things to their former state, with added insight and new dimension. To the Princes it meant a glorious phase of serendipity.

The other day I met for the first time Paul Leonard. It seems that just about everyone had heard or seen this unusual performer, but I must confess I knew nothing about him. He has been on the major networks, in stage shows, and countless school assemblies presenting his amazing program of bird calls and incredible bird sounds. His repertoire could run as high as a thousand imitations and variations of bird songs.

Those who hear Paul Leonard and applaud him usually say, "Well, he's gifted," or "He's a natural," or as one admirer facetiously remarked, "He was probably a bird of some kind in a previous incarnation."

Actually the Leonard story is the case of a man using the feed-forward formula. You see, Paul started out to be a trumpet player. That was his goal until his lips literally gave out under the strain and stress of overly-ambitious practicing. When a doctor said, "No more trumpet playing for you!" Paul stood face to face with an agonizing verdict. His bruised and broken lips seemed to have little to offer in the way of apocatastasis.

One day when he was exercising the muscles of his mouth and blowing air through his lips to cool the pain, he discovered that he was making whistling sounds, high-pitched, piercing metallic notes like the shrill call of a bird. Instantly there came the flash of a feed-forward formula. If he could learn to control those sounds, if he could develop this new technique, there could conceivably be a career in it. And that is exactly what happened. He began studying birds and learning bird songs and creating "bird rhapsodies," and today is the tomorrow he visualized when he stood in yesterday's ruins.

To catch on to this is to get the idea of the feed-forward formula.

When I said it is difficult to develop the art of apocatastasis, I was basing my opinion on personal experience. My ambition, as everyone who has heard my story knows, was to be a violinist, a real virtuoso, and to this end I had a fiddle under my chin at least four hours a day for some eight years. I had bought a $1500 violin on the installment plan and had it paid for, even though those were the penniless years of the Depression. That instrument was part of me. It gave direction to my life as a Seeing Eye dog gives direction to a blind man. I reached a point where I could play recitals—not Heifetz recitals by any means, but my Reindahl violin was no less precious to me than his Stradivarius was to him.

Fate, I was sure, had a great career in store for me. Then one night after playing a recital in a church (in "God's House," mind you) my precious instrument was stolen: case, bows, and all. When the word got out and the police got on the trail of the thief, when he realized how valuable the violin was, he tried to sell it, then to pawn it; and when these failed, he built a fire in a wooded area near a farmer's field and burned it.

Like Sabi Ben Suh, I had no insurance. I had no money. No one had any money in those days, and knowing nothing about apocatastasis, I found my days dismal and dark and spirit-broken. Did that end my violin career? It did. It ended then and there, but actually that was the moment when a larger career began opening for me. That was the turning point in my life.

Was the adjustment easy? It was tough. For a time I thought God and I would never make up again. Feedforward would have helped me, apocatastasis would have provided me with strength, and had I known some of the secrets out of the world of serendipity it would certainly have been more fun and considerably easier to play the game. I could at least have consoled myself with the knowledge that heartbreaks of some kind hit both the best and the worst of men, and that in them is always greater meaning than meets the eye.

For it was actually directly due to the theft of my violin that I got into a new and exciting field, the field of religious research. As I look back on it now, my apparent loss was my truly big break!

You need not be a sentimentalist to appreciate that the

greatest example of apocatastasis is found in the life of the Galilean. There is no more persuasive illustration than the recorded events of this Man's final earthly days. Who among those standing around the cross would have imagined that the climax to the crucifixion would be the resurrection, or who would have dreamed that out of a Friday tragedy would come a Sunday triumph?

"Did Jesus, on Golgotha, already know what would happen in the garden?" I have no answer to that one. No one has. I can take either side of the argument and make a case for it. All I know is that if light follows darkness, as this Biblical saga says, then we should by all odds have more confidence, hope, and trust when darksome moments come to us. In a very real way, no man escapes his Via Dolorosa or his Calvary, and the meaning of this is clear: neither can any man escape his Easter triumph.

The secret of apocatastasis is faith: faith in life, faith in our ultimate destiny, faith that if we do our best and leave the rest, in confidence, to Him who rules the universe, we will have done our part. The feed-forward formula insists there is an interlocking relationship between Him and us.

If this sort of thinking is a form of fatalism, make the most of it. Some of the best-adjusted people I know are fatalists. They have developed the art of inner resignation without losing the art of inner compassion. They are "modified fatalists" who know that an individual *can* do something about winning the battle against unseen forces. It is at exactly this point that their fatalism works wonders for them. They believe that when they have done their best, when they have exhausted their sincerest efforts or run their course of futility, then faith steps in to absorb fate, and the feed-forward formula begins its work.

A good example, and one of my inspirations during my playwriting days, was Eugene O'Neill. Some critics said his plays were fatalistic, but often when I got discouraged about the direction my life should take, I thought of him. For many years he did not know what he wanted to do with Eugene Gladstone O'Neill. His father insisted he go to Princeton and he did, only to flunk out after the second semester. Then he got married, only to be divorced twelve months later. So he went prospecting for gold, then sailed the seas as a stevedore, and then went to a sanitarium with a condition diagnosed as advanced tuberculosis.

People said this was the end. Actually it was the beginning. Down and out, O'Neill decided to be up and doing. His first full length, Pulitzer-prizewinning play, *Beyond the Horizon*, was literally born on a hospital bed. It was from here that the noted playwright went on to win two more Pulitzers and the rare honor of a Nobel prize for literature. For people of all time O'Neill serves as an example of the power waiting to be released in the feed-forward formula, projected from a low point of life to the high peak of creative expression.

If a loser can feed forward with a will to win, or a sick person with a will to be well, or a failure with a will to succeed, if a *mirza* can do it with a flooded house, or a trumpeter with a swollen lip, or a fiddler who lost his violin, and it works ... think how it will work for the winner or the well or the successful person who keeps in mind (if he can remember it) apocatastasis!

And the Princes said, "If only all men could learn the secret. If only everyone could remember the saying, 'Until tomorrow becomes today, men will be blind to the good fortune hidden in unfortunate acts.' "

15

MIND IS THE TRAVELER

$\mathcal{M}$y interest in serendipity prompts me to make a confession: Sometimes when I take a trip I don't know where I'm going.

It was not always this way. I used to plot and plan my itinerary step by step, convinced that anticipation is half the fun of traveling and perhaps it is. I used to insist on a fixed schedule, one that could be followed as meticulously as a guided tour, knowing where I would be almost every hour of every day, and letting my associates in on my time-track. My firm belief in serendipity has changed all that. I now leave my schedule open and flexible, knowing that chance is a most marvelous guide and that fate is usually waiting just around the bend.

Philosopher Lin Yutang went even further. He maintained that the best way to take a trip is not only not to know where you are going, but not to know where you have been when you get back. That may be carrying things too far, but the implication is that travel should permit room for destiny to play her part and lead the voyager into unforeseen adventures.

There should be an allowable overtone to travel in the same way that an orchestra accompanies a soloist in his recital. Better still, travel should be like the feeling we have at the end of a good day when we think not in terms of single moments but of the exciting montage of events that combined to make the day significant.

That is the way the three Princes of Serendip traveled, ready for the unexpected, tantalized by spontaneous happenings which they realized were part of the natural order of things.

The deeper import of this approach became clear one summer evening when the Princes stopped at an inn at the edge of the village of Kanah, in the land of Ephraim. When they checked in, the innkeeper sighed and said, "How I envy you your opportunity to travel! How I would like to see the Acropolis in Athens and the Agora which was the center of the old city, and the prison where Socrates drank the hemlock. It was really a cave, you know. How I long to gaze on the pyramids of Egypt, particularly Cheops, which is four hundred and fifty feet high, and Sakkara, oldest pyramid in the world. What wouldn't I give to walk the alcazar of the Moorish kings at Granada, the original of which was built of red stone, and red and white intermingling."

He talked this way at great length, mentioning historic scenes and giving such minute details about each that the Princes said, "How is it you lament your lack of travel, yet you speak of these places with greater knowledge than people who have been there?"

"Oh," moaned the innkeeper, "I travel only vicariously by way of travelers who stop here as guests. I travel by things I hear and things I read."

"Be grateful for that!" said the Princes. "Mind is the best of all travelers."

Then they went on to explain that, as in physical travel, one should have an open-ended schedule, so in mental travel one should by all means have an open mind (as, of course, the innkeeper presumably had despite his make-believe grumbling).

It seems to me an excellent observation, this bit of princely advice. By all means, let your mind take a trip. I do not mean a hallucinogenic trip over which you have no control or an alcoholic binge which sends you you know not where, but a "thought trip" in which you open your mind to creative ideas or invoke the inflow of something superconscious. Instruct your mind to be prepared to run into new acquaintances and to be ready to meet strangers unawares. I mean acquaintances and strangers of the mental realm. As there are new adventures and new people waiting along the travel trail, so there are new ideas ready to reveal themselves to the unbiased traveler of the mind.

For example, one of the scientists who has contributed exciting data and uncanny speculation about the composition of the moon got into the lunar and space program by his study of conditions at the bottom of the sea! He is J. J. Gilvarry, consultant on the staff of the Rand Corporation.

"The moon," he reported in a *Saturday Review* article, "was far from my consciousness when one of my assignments after World War II directed me to calculate the most effective method of blasting a hole deep enough to get at buried and heavily shielded submarine pens."

During an experiment on the sea floor he learned that a crater at that level caused by an explosion is considerably less than the same crater on dry land. Relating this theory to the craters on the moon and following this line of reasoning, he concluded that there must have been a time when there were seas of water on the moon.

In speaking of the steps by which his thinking traveled from sea bottom to lunar surface, Gilvarry said, "The circumstances are worth detailing because they illustrate the roundabout route over which science often travels in arriving at destinations it never chose."

Serendipity, pure and simple! Mind is the traveler if you will but give it latitude and keep an open schedule as far as new thoughts are concerned.

Now this suggestion to permit the mind to travel freely may be contrary to things we have been taught and may run counter to certain meditative practices which advise us to get hold of a word or a concept and concentrate on it, shaking off any extraneous thoughts that may intrude. We have all been warned at times *not* to let the mind wander. I was taught in both church and school: "Keep your mind on this. Concentrate on this one idea." In the world of serendipity, however, mind realizes it may profit from woolgathering.

The Princes of Serendip were bold enough to suggest the value of daydreaming, fantasizing, supposing, reasoning, speculating, and these are modes of travel that we all too often rule out. *Think*, and you will immediately be on a trip. Mind is the traveler.

The therapy and adventure involved in thought-travel can easily be proved. I put it to an acid test recently when after a wearying airflight I was caught, along with other passengers, in a holding operation over Chicago's O'Hare airport. The bottleneck at O'Hare is known to every pilot and passenger and here we were circling the field for an hour and a half, round and round in the monotonous flight pattern with the incessant drone of the jet intensifying our impatience and causing a fellow passenger to proclaim, "It's like they say, if you have time to spare, go by air!"

I decided to employ the time by doing some thought-travel. Even though the plane was going in circles and getting nowhere, my thoughts were unbound by any holding order. I could travel where I wished—mentally. I went backward in thought, reliving other flights I had taken, and was amazed at the mass of half-forgotten information stored in my memory file. I went forward in thought to future flights, thrilled at all the unfinished plans I had.

Suddenly the man in the seat next to me, with whom I had conversed little during the trip, began to laugh softly to himself. I looked at him with some apprehension, wondering if our overly-long carousel was getting through to him.

"It's a funny thing," he said to me. "I just had a revelation."

"That so?" I ventured.

"Yes," he said lucidly, "I just made a decision. For weeks now I have been trying to decide between two jobs that have been offered me. I've been going in circles like this plane. Now all of a sudden I've made up my mind. I know definitely which job I'm going to take."

"Well, good," I said, but in my heart I was thinking how serendipity plays its part, and I was wanting to ask him whether he thought he would have made the decision if we had landed on time and not been trapped in the air for so long. Perhaps he was wondering the same thing himself.

Let your mind wander and see what happens. You can make your own experiment. Put this book aside for a moment, close your eyes and think of something. Anything. For example, a bird. Sit quietly. Think of a bird and see where the thought of the bird takes you. In less than a minute your thoughts will have traveled meaningfully backward and forward through time and space. It could be that a great new idea will come to you.

Try the experiment on a friend, as I did recently on my wife. I said, "Think of something and see where your mind takes you." Always happy to cooperate with me in my eccentricities, she said, "I'll think of a flower. Is a flower okay?"

"Anything is okay," I said. "Close your eyes."

"I see a daisy," she mused. "It is in a field of daisies on a beautiful hillside. It is like hundreds of other daisies and they are all facing the sun. Now a butterfly comes and lights on this particular daisy. It rests there and sways on the flower. It is all very pretty. All the daisies seem to be watching. I think of the butterfly and remember that I came from a cocoon, from a caterpillar. I think of immortality and the cycle of things. Everything that lives, dies and is reborn. That is what it seems like to me just now. The butterfly flies away. A little girl comes through the daisy patch. I see myself in this girl. She picks the daisy and runs away with it, laughing and happy. The daisy reminds me of other flowers and all the occasions at which flowers were used, occasions that figured in my life, and I remember the first flowers you ever gave me."

This went on into a lengthy mental expedition. I daresay that you can begin with any thought, with any event in your life, and discover that thinking triggers thinking into unusual and even mystical fields. In letting your mind travel, you give serendipity a chance to work in the realm of thought, as it does in the area of physical travel when you are taking a trip. Properly approached, it brings us deeper tranquility and an added insight into life.

One of my favorite recollections is of a visit I had with an elderly Hutterite woman in the Bon Homme Colony near Tabor, South Dakota. The Hutterite people, who live communally, separated and set apart from "the world," are averse to travel. Most of them are born and live and die without wandering from the commune physically or straying mentally from the Hutterian belief that "the world" with its wars, violence, and crime is Satan's habitat. Yet I never fail to marvel at the wealth of information these people, like the innkeeper of Kanah, carry around in their seemingly closed minds.

I had returned from a global tour and was visiting the Bon Homme settlement. Here sat this typically resigned Hutterian woman in her rocking chair, calmly knitting. Her polka dot headscarf framed her serene and thoughtful face. She could have been the model for Whistler's Mother, and she rocked quietly and knitted while I regaled her with stories of the places I had been and the things I had seen. With quiet knowing she occasionally filled in a detail or contributed a winsome bit of obscure information. When I finally finished my storytelling, she looked at me wistfully and said with a smile, "You have been in all those places and now you are here. I haven't been anywhere but I am here, too."

Is it possible, I wonder, that there exists a pool of consciousness, a reservoir of information into which we can dip mentally and get our knowledge without even pausing in our rocking and our knitting? It would seem so, when we consider how much wisdom we have, the source of which is unknown—wisdom and knowledge that have come to us by way of some process of cosmic osmosis. The thought opens up a fascinating inner world for travel. New discoveries lie latent within us, not "out there somewhere" but within our individual reach of mind.

Mind is the traveler. One thought triggers another. Ideas come into being just as strangers come into our life during physical travel. There is no limit as to where you can go in this adventure of thought-travel and there is no restriction on the creative breakthrough that may come to you. As a man thinketh in his *heart* so is he, but as he thinketh in his *mind* so shall he be.

I have a hunch that when the innkeeper told the Princes he envied them their continual traveling, he may have had his tongue in his cheek, knowing what he knew.

16

WHILE MORTALS SLEEP

In the annals of animal lore there are few clearer examples of a serendipitous happening than the fantasy recounted by songwriter Johnny Marks in his universally famous Christmas canticle, "Rudolph the Red-Nosed Reindeer."

Here are all the ingredients in the theories perpetually advanced by the Princes of Serendip. First of all we have Rudolph, a fellow who never got the breaks, an underdog (or an underdeer, so to say) with a nose unlike the normal noses of his breed. Secondly, all counts are against him. Socially he is a misfit. Psychologically he has a problem. But somewhere deep in his reindeer heart lurks a mystique that says, "Even if you cannot reach a stated goal, there may be other goals equally as important somewhere along the way."

Came the foggy night. Came the call from earth summoning Santa. Came the break for Rudolph, whose shining nose paid off as the lightbearer and the wayshower for Santa's legendary team. Long before Rudolph was ever immortalized and ages before Saint Nick had reindeer and a sled, the Princes of Serendip had a saying, "Serendipity is involved in all life, at all times, as part of nature's law."

Many a touching fable has been written about animals and the unexpected acclaim that came to them serendipitously. There are stories about a burro, rejected for being too docile for any good. He was pawned off on a man called Joseph and eventually bore upon his somber back the "Mother of God" on her way to Bethlehem.

There is the legend about a camel that didn't have a beggarman's chance to become famous but was chosen by Mohammed to bear the Prophet in triumph to the holy city of Mecca. There was the lowly steed that pulled the chariot that brought the Buddha out of the confinement of his father's palace, and the dog that became a companion to the prophet Zoroaster, and there were the animals of the forest who, hunted by men, became the special wards of St. Francis. In these and other legends is a response that tells us that we, too, are serendipitously involved in the laws of chance . . . and that very often, while mortals sleep, other creatures of earth know that mystery and magic are woven into the pattern of life, even though it may be nothing more than the honor of guiding Santa's sleigh through the uncharted skyways of a murky Christmas Eve.

Take, for example, the story of Fija, a German police dog that went to school to become a Seeing Eye dog and flunked the course. It seems she had trouble passing the traffic tests. She could lead and love her trainer under average circumstances but when it came to crowded streets and blinking lights and the noise of cars, she was undone. Obviously, Fija was a country dog and might have done well for a sightless man who never strayed from his rural habitat, but diplomas are not granted that way. Fija was a dropout.

She sat in her kennel cage as philosophically as she could, realizing, I suppose, that she had much or little to be thankful for, depending on whom she compared herself with. She took exercise periods and romped reflectively in the runway as if the world had mysteries to be solved, but anyone with half a heart for dogs could sense the sadness in her moist brown eyes as she gazed out through the wire meshes of her cage. Sometimes at night she dreamed (at least she trembled in her sleep), and often she stood for a time looking into the dark, wondering no doubt about the little ironies of life. Fija had failed her finals.

I met Fija after she got out of the kennels. I met her in a farmyard in Kootenay country, Canada, where we have our cabin. When I drove into the yard there stood this splendid, defiant dog, daring me to get out of the car unannounced. I didn't get out. I honked and waited until a youngster, about six years of age, appeared and threw his arms around the dog. "Fija won't hurt you," he said. "She's too sweet. She's smart, too. Sit, Fija. Stay, Fija."

Fija sat. Fija stayed. Fija had found a home and I heard the story of how she had failed at the Seeing Eye School and how the Canadian couple had got her at the kennels, a perfect companion for Andy, their young son. Fija was also good at rounding up the cows and she was a competent watchdog, but no one ever mentioned in her presence the fact that she hadn't made it academically or that she had not really reached her goal in life.

Then a short time after my visit, there came a night, a

Kootenay night when the air was still and a sense of extreme quiet hung over the valley. Fija was asleep on the back porch of the farmhouse when she smelled smoke. Then she saw flames breaking through a corner of the house. She began to bark and claw frantically at the door. Smoke was pouring out of the house when Andy's parents stumbled into the yard. They tried unsuccessfully to go back in and rescue their child, and it was then that Fija found her moment of greatness. She dove into the billows of smoke and came back dragging the frightened child to safety. Did she tell herself, I wonder, that though she had failed to handle the mystery of blinking traffic signals she had learned the art of finding her way through smoke and flames to play the hero's part?

Thank you, Fija, for a lesson in serendipity.

You can talk about shepherds and wise men and even about angels singing in the radiance of a shining star, but the first outsiders who saw the Bethlehem Babe and heard His cry were four-footed friends who shared with Him the homey warmth and sheltered presence of the enchanted manger. No wonder legend has it that on Christmas Eve the cattle speak a common language and confide to one another the secrets of this Holy Night.

Speaking of dogs reminds me of a story that began in St. Petersburg several years ago when I was on a lecture tour. A well-known Unity minister, Louise Beaty, had a wire-haired terrier. I had one, too, but Louise's was disciplined and docile while mine was something of a problem child.

"How did you train your dog to be so well-mannered?" I asked.

"It wasn't difficult," Louise told me. "Whenever he did something he wasn't supposed to do, instead of scolding him I said, 'You are God's little dog, and God's little dog is gentle and kind.' So he just naturally got to be gentle and kind."

Well, it was worth a try, I thought, and gradually the idea got hold of me and worked its way into my treatment of Mike, my wire-haired terrier.

One day I looked out my study window. Mike was gaily ripping up a pillow which my wife had put out into the spring sunshine for airing. The feathers were flying and my impulse was to deal with this rampaging terrier with a rolled-up newspaper or some equally effective weapon. But something said to me, "He's God's little dog." It was rather disconcerting actually, but after a while, when my wife had dealt in womanly fashion with the incident and had gathered most of the feathers together, I noticed a remarkable sequel to the occurrence. Several birds were picking up the stray feathers, presumably for use in building their nests. God's little dog had serendipitously provided some soft and fleecy texture for God's little birds. This much, at least, was obvious, and who was to say that the Princes were wrong when they affirmed, "Serendipity is involved in all life, at all times, as a part of nature's law"?

It is consoling for me to think that occasionally I, too, may be an effective instrument in the fate and fortune of someone else. To be aware of this is a great discovery. All too often we feel we must always be on the receiving end of things. We must "get something out of it." We must be the beneficiaries. But the truth is that in nature's scheme of things we are also to be contributors to others. Do not try to understand this in order to have faith, but have faith in this in order to better understand the whole of life.

I am not quite sure about the state of consciousness in animals. Some evolutionists insist that life had to reach the status of *homo sapiens* before it attained even *self*-consciousness. They say that animals cannot stand apart and look at themselves objectively. I often wonder. I have a hunch they know more about life and death than they will ever admit, and surely they live in highly sensory worlds, worlds of taste and smell and sound which are practically closed to us. They have extrasensory perception, as I realized again recently when I ran across "Thinking Animals" by Karl Krall and read again the amazing account of Kluge Hans.

Here was the story of a Russian stallion, serendipitously purchased by a Prussian eccentric, Wilhelm-von-Osten. Perhaps the horse was content to be owned by anyone just so he could follow his natural mating instinct, but knowing the temperament of Wilhelm, the stallion may well have felt that such ownership left much to be desired. Nonetheless, Wilhelm had a hunch that the stallion had some special, secret capabilities other than biological urges, and one day he set out to prove his theory.

He set a bowling pin in front of the sturdy steed, then forcibly raised the stallion's right hoof and set it down emphatically to the count of "one." Soon whenever he placed the bowling pin, the horse of its own volition would count "one" with a determined beat of its foot. Wilhelm went on to train it to count any number of bowling pins and soon the horse became so adept it was dubbed Kluge Hans (Hans-the-smart-one).

With German tenacity Wilhelm-von-Osten substituted a blackboard and wrote down numerals in place of the bowling pins. Soon Kluge Hans was counting the written figures. Next he began doing addition and subtraction and then, according to testimony of reliable witnesses including Maurice Maeterlinck, Hans proceeded to make several arithmetical deductions, unassisted by his trainer.

Nor was this the end of the story. Having broken through the psychic barrier of animal consciousness, Hans and several other horses of the Elberfeld stables were solving problems bordering on calculus. Kluge Hans became so fantastic at reasoning by use of symbols that von-Osten was accused of diabolic persuasion, trickery, and hypnotism, but the story stands authenticated in the annals of animalry. Every time you go to a circus you will see telltale signs that somewhere in the subliminal awareness of horses, dogs, cats, seals, dolphins, and what-have-you there lurk limitless aptitudes which need only a greater capability on the part of man to release them. For it is a well-known saying that to train an animal, one must first know more than the animal knows.

At any rate, the rhythmic hooves of Kluge Hans still sound along the serendipity road and all our logic-chopping resistance will not break down the fact that "Serendipity is involved in all life, at all times as part of nature's law."

These "chance happenings" in animals prove something deep and inexplicable in man. As in the case of Kluge Hans it may be that we, too, often feel possessed and caught by situations beyond our control. We are subjected to training against our will. Figuratively someone sets a symbol before us and says, "Count!" forcing us to respond as if to a conditioned reflex. We may think of our jobs, our associates, or even our friends as persistent trainers. But there comes a time when by a leap in consciousness the miracle occurs, the gap is bridged, and an unrealized potential convinces us that there was special meaning and a cause behind the experiences.

I feel this way about Fija and I have something of an affinity with her, for there are courses I have flunked and goals I have not reached. Sometimes while other mortals sleep, I wake from my dreaming and in the stillness wonder about the way of things. But there are also moments when, like the dropout, I feel an inner stirring of achievement and something tells me I am in the right place at the right time, even if it means going through a bit of smoke and flames.

There is also Rudolph, and may there always be a Christmas! Christmas, serendipitously speaking, is that moment of divine birth in every individual when he can play a special part in self-discovery. Rest assured there will come a time when your talent will be called upon to play its role. Who is to say that you may not, like Rudolph, "go down in history"?

17
EVER THE MOON

*E*ver since man's first decision to explore outer space, someone has raised the question, "What's the good of it?" The spectacular achievement of an astronaut's scraping boot on the pockmarked lunar surface did not provide the entire answer, and there are those who point out that every pound of rock collected by the intrepid moon-walkers cost America $400,000,000. The argument is that there is so much to accomplish on Planet Earth in the way of peace and plenty that top priority should be given to earthlings and their needs, and we should let the moon alone.

The countercharge by those who favor moon shots and advocate voyages to other planets and the distant stars is that there are enough benefits to justify any expenditure and vindicate any risk: hospitals in the sky, minerals and precious metals, fresh living space and new frontiers, to say nothing of immortality. There is already a new slogan: "If you can live until the turn of the century, you can live forever."

Both opponents and promoters of the space effort are strangely silent on one phase of the program, one which we feel should by all means be given attention: the thing called serendipity.

This is the crux of the matter as far as the value of space exploration is concerned. It is also the very crux of *life*. Most of us are where we are, have what we have, and are on the way to becoming what we will be, because of something serendipitous. An unmarked turn in the road, a coincidental meeting, a sudden encounter, an unexpected circumstance, an accidental happening—these and the purling touch of fate have landed most of us in our present situations. Serendipitists are of the opinion that these occurrences have lost the implication of chance and are actually part of the order of things. They are persuaded that we as individuals do not make these unforeseen contingencies; they are made for us and woven into our destiny out of the loom of life.

That is why, in a consideration of extraterrestrial programming, we should not overlook the fact of serendipity. Who can say where it will lead or what will be found locked in the silent heart of the moon or on Mars? You cannot tell, any more than you can predict the potential of a newborn child or foretell what will happen to you on your next adventure.

Nowhere do we get a clearer view of the serendipitous "extras" than in the history of exploration and travel. Figuratively, there has always been a "moon," and someone has always insisted on reaching it. There have always been moon-watchers and moon-explorers, and the Apollo flights have helped close the gap between the two while serendipity rewarded each graciously and with patience for their points of view.

First of all, they were assured that a seemingly divided America could pool its know-how and get things done. They found new faith in our way of life. They learned that great events have a unifying influence, that the spirit of the entire world is stirred by daring achievements, and that a spiritual and philosophical undertone moves just below the surface of most of humankind.

One of the earliest "moonstruck adventurers" who made world news was Marco Polo. The "moon" swimming enticingly in geographical space in his day (1254-1324) was Cathay (China)—as unexplored, unvisited, and mysterious a "planet" as any that dangled in the Oriental sky. To many a medieval observer, Cathay was mythological; to the Venetians who were Marco Polo's people, it was a forbidding and faraway land. The man in this "moon" was equally mysterious. He was known as Kublai Khan and his empire extended from China through Persia into Russia, comprising roughly half of the civilized world. Marco, seventeen, urged his father and an uncle (who were seasoned travelers) to take him with them on a great adventure halfway around the world—a world that some people even doubted was round—to Cathay and Kublai Khan.

By ship, by camelback, by elephant, by oxcart, and on foot they made their journey. Months and years went by, and more than one Venetian must have said, "What's the good of it?"

Some insisted that the goal of Marco Polo's trip was commerce and trade, and perhaps as far as Marco's father, a merchantman, was concerned, it was. But serendipity tells another story. The voyage, which covered twenty-three years (three years going, seventeen years with Kublai Khan, and three years returning), had fringe benefits that changed the course of history.

Through the dramatic description of his journey, his homemade maps of hitherto unknown regions, his record of people and places never before visited or explored, his theories of travel, such a wealth of information and inspiration was forthcoming that the world was never quite the same again.

And speaking of serendipity, it is a matter of record that Marco Polo's adventures would never have been reported as thoroughly as they were had it not been for an unexpected and coincidental circumstance. Here is what happened: On his return to Venice, Marco became a naval officer, and in a battle with the Genoese was taken captive. A prisoner of war, he shared a cell with a soldier from Pisa named Rustichello, a professional writer of romances. What could be more serendipitous than a meeting of this kind, at which a would-be author (Marco) and a ghost writer (Rustichello) were thrown together into confinement?

It is doubtful whether *The Book of Marco Polo* would ever have seen the light of day but for (a) the decision of the adventurer to become a navy man, (b) his chance capture by the Genoese, (c) the coincidence of his sharing the same prison with a writer, and (d) the rare ability of Rustichello to put the travel material into dramatic form (for without his touch it would have been dry as lunar dust).

What was the good of it? Well, there is substantial evidence that without *The Book of Marco Polo* another historic serendipitous saga might never have found its way into our history books, at least not in the sequences so familiar to us. For without the daring Venetian's trip to

China, Columbus might never have attempted to set sail for what turned out to be the discovery of another world.

Take a good look at this serendipitous phase of exploration. What Columbus was actually interested in was finding a short route to the Cathay he had read about in Marco Polo's narrative. A Latin version of the book by Rustichello had appeared in the early 1300s and young Christopher Colombo (1451-1506), son of a Spanish-Jewish weaver of Genoa, got hold of a treasured copy. He devoured this as he did other "travel books" and filled it with copious marginal notes. Marco had gone to China by land; Columbus was determined to go by sea, for at this period in history sailing vessels were the "spacecraft" that possessed the mind of man with the fantastic speculation that it was possible to go east by traveling west.

The persistency and audacity of Columbus in getting support for his dream to sail to China and India need not concern us here. The important point is that he was "moonstruck" with the fever of new discovery. That he was only thirty-three when he implored the king of Portugal to outfit him with money and ships (and was turned down), that he was thirty-five when he persuaded the Spanish royal couple, Ferdinand and Isabella, to underwrite his venture, are of passing interest (even the pure fiction that the queen pawned her jewels to raise the necessary funds).

What concerns us here is serendipity. Moonstruck, Columbus became impatient with the dillydallying of the Spanish rulers and was about ready to try elsewhere, when he chanced to meet a friend who told him to seek an audience with the king and queen once more. He did, and it was because of this chance meeting with a persuasive friend that a trio of ships eventually sailed out of Palos, Spain, under Columbus' command.

Well-wishers and skeptics gave him a dubious farewell. Some self-styled soothsayers said the ships would never make it because even if the earth was round, there must be a falling-off place. Furthermore, the sea was an enemy, they warned, not a friend, and there were strange and jealous gods that ruled the waves. So they watched the ships "blast off" and sail out of sight: the decked *Santa Maria* a mere 117 feet in length, the two caravels, the *Nina* and the *Pinta*, measuring a scant 50 feet each. And as the crowd turned away from the restless sea that washed this port of southern Spain, more than one bystander must have said, "What's the good of it?"

One good of it was serendipity.

Columbus never reached his goal, neither India nor Cathay nor the Asian mainland. There is still debate as to whether he ever saw the mainland of "America." But because of him the gateway to an uncharted continent opened, and the Bahamas, the West Indies, and at least a seaman's sight of Cuba were serendipitous rewards for his adventure.

"In my enterprise," he reported to Ferdinand and Isabella shortly before his death, "neither reason nor mathematics nor maps were of any use to me. Fully accomplished were the words of Isaiah, 'In that day the Lord will extend his hand yet a second time to recover the remnant which is left of his people . . . from the coastlands of the sea.' "

He had to believe that chance is part of divine order, as every adventurer eventually discovers. After all, in looking back over his life Columbus was impressed by the fact that his first arrival in Portugal was in itself serendipitous. As a young corsair he was attached to a ship which caught fire off the Portuguese coast. At that time he swam to shore and found that he had landed amazingly close to a school of navigation. He took this as a sign to become a navigator, and never returned to his home in Genoa again.

After his death, however, the "moon" remained, which is to say that the new lands he claimed for Spain merely whetted man's interest for other, greater discoveries. The geographical universe was still unknown and the passage to Cathay was yet to be found.

As far as the discovery of the "New World" is concerned, it is generally conceded that Norsemen had already set foot on this continent nearly five hundred years before Columbus appeared on the scene, but it remained for a strange twist of serendipity to give the country a name. Why was it eventually called America, and not "Norseland" or "Columbo" or even "Isabella," when it was finally sighted by Spanish captains from their bases in the Caribbean?

The answer again is serendipity. A young Italian named Amerigo Vespucci (1451-1512) wanted to be a seaman, but his parents persuaded him to become a banker. This was a bitter pill for Vespucci, but he made the most of it. He became a banker but spent his evenings in navigational study and entered vicariously into the adventures of men who roamed the seas.

Then one day in 1491 his employer sent Vespucci to Seville to straighten out a financial matter with a merchant named Giannotto Berardi. When Vespucci arrived at the Berardi office he discovered that his client was engaged in outfitting ships and had as one of his customers Christopher Columbus. This unexpected and exciting turn of events eventually brought Columbus and Vespucci together (circa 1495), and together they dreamed of other worlds.

When, after the death of Berardi, Vespucci became manager of the Seville agency, what should be more logical than that he, a banker skilled in the points of the transit and compass, embark on voyages to the West Indies? In 1501, when he was forty-seven years of age (five years before the passing of Columbus), Vespucci embarked on his own expedition under Portuguese auspices. Early in 1502 his ship touched a great continent, not the Asian mainland which others had sought and never found, but a vast hemisphere, a new world, an exciting "planet" in the drifting ocean of water and space. In 1507, a year after Columbus' death, the name *America* (in honor of Amerigo Vespucci) appeared in print in Spain and Portugal for the first time.

"What's the good of it?"

Who is to say? Only those who have the heart and spirit of a Marco Polo, a Columbus, a Vespucci, or who are stirred by the exploits of an unnamed Norseman or a Velazquez or a Ponce de Leon, a De Soto, a Cabot, a Drake, a Champlain, a Magellan, a Neil Armstrong . . . or even you or me.

So get on with your adventure and your quest. You may not always find what you seek, but you may discover something equally great, or greater, in the scheme of things.

Serendipity: the gift of finding valuable or agreeable things not actually sought for.

Yesterday, a new continent. Today, outer space. Ever the moon!

18

THE WRONG SIDE
OF RIGHT

*D*uring a lecture tour in the Philadelphia area I was invited by a friend to visit a famous synagogue in Jenkintown. The midweek morning was damp and dreary and as we approached the building my friend and I agreed that architecturally the synagogue certainly justified its name: Mt. Sinai. Through the fog it was spectacular. Frank Lloyd Wright had done his talented best to give the structure the shape and semblance of the mountain of the Lord. Inside we were welcomed by the rabbi who was happy to show us around. I noticed a number of plastic pails of various colors set about the sanctuary and when I inquired as to the nature of the holy day that was to be observed, the rabbi said, "Holy Day, my eye! The roof leaks!"

He went on to explain that the complex symmetry of the structure presented a problem. Considerable money had been spent on trying to remedy the situation but still the rain came trickling through. They had complained to Mr. Wright about it after the annoyance was discovered but the eccentric Wisconsin architect retorted impatiently, "Who complains about a little water on Mt. Sinai!"

The account interested me because I once lived in the neighborhood of Spring Green, Wisconsin, where the noted architect had his famous Taliesen, the home which he once described to me as "an eyebrow on a hill." I was young at the time and was often amused by the man's acid-headed temper and searing tongue. Some people said that to take note only of his temperament, however, was to see the wrong side of Wright. I am now prepared to go even further than that. Without this apparently wrong side of Wright, there might not have been such an impressive right side.

After all, he was a genius. Everyone knew that the Imperial Hotel in Tokyo which he designed had withstood the devastating earthquake in 1923 when other buildings toppled and 143,000 people were killed. I remember when I stayed at the Imperial I bumped my head on many a doorway. Wright would probably have said, "Learn to duck. If you were Japanese you wouldn't be so tall."

The wrong side of Wright was really not so wrong when you remembered the right side. And to bring this down to cases, I ask myself how often I fail to see the right side of people because I am so critical of what I construe as the wrong side according to my particular standard of judgment. Sometimes the pails we see are not there for any particular holy day. It may be raining.

There is another side to this wrong-side, right-side equation and this is where serendipity comes in. The

Princes of Serendip insisted that anyone with half an eye could see the wrong side, but that an inner eye was needed to properly discern the right side. In this they would definitely have agreed with a master Teacher who on His peripatetic tours in Palestine had a neat way of seeing the commonly unseen. It was not always easy for the average individual to go along with Him in His reasoning, but He put the challenge up to them just the same.

One day His disciples called his attention to a blind man. "Who sinned that this man should be sightless?" they asked. "He or his parents?" The master Teacher said, "Neither. But that the glory of the Lord might be revealed." And He healed him.

He had a way of making men look within themselves with an inner eye to see the possibility of the other side of things and what He was trying to do was emphasize the right side of wrong as well as see beyond the wrong side of right. On one occasion He said something about turning the other cheek, as if to suggest that when you give an assailant the shock treatment of kindness and submission you might conceivably inspire him into a change of attitude. Few people believed Him in His day and few believe Him today, but somehow we all have a hunch that an approach of this kind is basically sound if someone only had the courage to try it and the right kind of personality to back it up. At a deep feeling level we are persuaded that there is a good side to almost every wrongdoer and the chance that there is something right in a bad situation if we could dig deeply enough into the apparent wrong.

Lacking the perfect will to follow through on some of these challenging precepts, we have developed a facility of rationalizing our way around them. You may recall the character in *Our Town* who had this to say about the turn-the-other-cheek philosophy:

"You say you ought to give a bad man a chance to do more bad to you, like giving him your other cheek to slap? I wonder. If you do pure good to a man that's harmed you, that shames him too much. No man is so bad he ought to be shamed that way. Do you see? You ought to do just a little bad to him in return so that he can keep his self-respect. See what I mean?"

A friend of mine who engages in what he facetiously calls a "spiritual cleanup week" every once in a while, as a sort of purgation, shared his utopian overlist with me one day. He is quite an average man, an accountant, married, father of two grown daughters, a fairly good churchman, middle of the road politically and all that, and three or four times a year he seriously observes these special days. Others have their diet weeks, or fun weeks, or get-away-from-it-all weeks, he has this period of ultra-religious goodness. During these special days he devotes himself to long meditation periods, eats no meat, drinks no coffee, reads only inspirational literature, turns off his TV and tries to follow his utopian overlist in which he has ten special commandments:

1. The goodness of every person is in direct ratio to the goodness you are willing to find in him.
2. Your estimate of another person is the preform that shapes his character.
3. The wrong method in the hands of the right person can prove to be right.
4. The right method in the hands of the wrong person can prove to be wrong.
5. If you are limited to a five minute interview prepare for it in ten minutes of silent meditation.

6. The greatest blessing lacking in life is the willingness to see our blessings.
7. Love a person for what he is.
8. Love him again for what he is not.
9. Love him again for what he may become.
10. Love him once more for not judging you as you are judging him.

I have always been intrigued by this friend of mine and it is interesting to conjecture on people's opinions of him. If they met him during his "holy week," some would surely be greatly impressed. If they met him when he is under pressure, they would get another reaction. But something out of "spiritual cleanup week" rubs off on him and through the years I have seen him mellow and grow more like the list he has so assiduously prepared.

Which prompts me to the conclusion that there is clearly a right side even to what you might construe as the wrong side of his right. An old book on Hinduism once told me that a person becomes what he is in the eyes of the beholder. Ask a husband to describe his spouse and he will obviously do so as he sees her in her role as wife. The child, however, will see her as a mother. The boss for whom she works sees her as an employee. Her hair dresser sees her as a client. Her housekeeper sees her as a mistress, and so on. Though she is the same woman, everyone sees her differently. And the interesting thing is that we ourselves see ourselves differently, too. Who is the real you?

The Princes of Serendip must have had some of these things in mind when they talked about the inner eye. If you can see the right side in yourself when you happen to do wrong and when you can find a lesson in this wrong side of right, you have learned to walk the serendipity road.

In fact, how else can you grow? You grow through adversity no less than through the pleasantries of life. You grow as you learn to see yourself from all sides with an eye that is "single," an inner eye.

Some years ago I planted a maple seedling near our cabin in British Columbia. It is on a promontory overlooking the lake and it never occurred to me that it was in the direct path of the wind coming with full force from every which way. My heart went out to that fledgling tree during many a storm when it was whipped practically to the ground and slashed unmercifully by a northwester. It shook and trembled and sometimes I thought I could hear it hold back a cry. But it always came back. It always straightened itself when the winds died down, squared its branches, and stood up stronger and more confident than before. One summer it got some strange bugs on its branches. They cut into its tender bark and it began to shed its leaves. A visitor said, "It's had it. Cut it down." He didn't know the tree. He didn't have the inner eye. He hadn't seen it stand up to the elements. He only saw the wrong side. Came a day when the bugs gave up and now even the wind shows more respect when it blows our way. I don't think that maple tree fears anything excepting a woodman's axe or fire perhaps.

I have concluded that there are many maple trees walking around. People, I mean. I often meet them in my travels, people who have borne the whiplash of fate and felt the winds of adversity, as the poet would say, and who are straighter and stronger because of their experiences. They may not get their names in the news. They do not make the lists of "our most noteworthy notables." They may not be honored as the citizens of the year. But there they are and whenever I meet them they challenge me to square my shoulders and lift my head and meet the universe on its own terms. And when I do this, even the things that "bug" me give up, and occasionally I reach a point where I fear nothing, not even fire or the woodsman's axe.

The assignment is to see beyond the wrong side of right, for there is so much that seems unfair, unjust, and deceptive in the world around me. There are so many times I catch myself saying, "Now, if I were running the universe. . . ." The lines out of an old song go hauntingly through my mind, "Right forever on the scaffold, wrong forever on the throne!" I would really have to give up if I believed that, if I went no further than that. What would I have left to stand on if this were true?

This is where the inner eye of serendipity comes in. It has a unique spiritualized peripheral vision. It tries to see life total, whole, complete. It looks beyond the wrong side and recognizes with unerring insight, the right side. Incredible what a man can see with this serendipitous eye! So incredible that some people with only two eyes call it fantasy, delusion, and naiveté.

But even the songwriter saw it. He took another look at truth and rightness dangling on the gallows and instead of seeing what most men saw, he grabbed his pen (which some say is mightier than the sword) and said, "Yet that scaffold sways the future! And behind the still unknown, standeth God within the shadows, keeping watch above His own!" And if I understand "His own" correctly that means every one of us and everything that God has made.

The Princes of Serendip had an intriguing point of view about our ability to see the right side of wrong and to penetrate beyond the wrong into the side of right.

They said, "There is never a time when we fully understand this, there are only moments when we *know*."

That is why I liked Mt. Sinai. And colored pails. And rain on the roof. And Holy Days, and maple trees, and a

Galilean walking. And spiritual cleanup weeks. And even doorways against which occasionally I bump my head.

19
THE OTHER SIDE
OF BUT

*T*he Princes of Serendip would
have appreciated my Aunt
Selma. I did. She never resented my occasional references
to her in my books, and her innocent unawareness of
certain influences in her life was refreshing. She had a few
kinks to iron out, as she often said, and one of these
would, I am sure, have intrigued the three Princes.

For a long time Aunt Selma had a habit of saying, "It
was all right, *but* . . . ." Then she would go into a
lamentation about what was wrong with a situation.

For example, after she went to a sale at a store and was
asked about it, she said, "It was all right, *but* the bargains
were gone."

"How was the movie you went to, Aunt Selma?"

"It was good, *but* it should have had a different ending."

"How was the church service, Aunt Selma?"

"Not too bad, *but* the songs surely didn't fit the sermon."

We all lived to see Aunt Selma get on the other side of "but" and that is why the Princes would have admired her.

What changed her? She never gave any better reason than that she just got to thinking. She got to thinking and there came a day when she looked at life through different eyes and put her sentences into inverted syntax.

Came a day when she returned from a sale at a store and said, "All the bargains were gone, *but* it was fun just the same."

"How was the movie, Aunt Selma?"

"It should have had a different end, *but* it was wonderful."

"How was the church service?"

"The songs didn't fit the sermon, *but* I got some good out of it anyway."

The other side of but.

This is one of the deep secrets of serendipity. What the Princes were trying to get across to people was not only that so-called chance, coincidence, and the unexpected are part of the natural order of things; they hoped to impress us with the truth that our personalities are shaped by our points of view. While serendipity means finding joy and meaning in discoveries on the way to a stated goal, the secret is to look upon *incidental* goals as substantial and upon accidental happenings as purposeful. It is a matter of syntax, not of language only, but of life.

To reverse your point of view is to start your life anew. A difference is effected in attitude and act if instead of saying, "It is good to be alive, but we cannot live forever," we learn to say, "We cannot live forever, but it is good to be alive." The first "but" implies fatalism, the second gives hint of a sense of radiant hope. The first affirms and then denies, the second denies and then erases the denial with an affirmation. Consider Emerson's famous saying, "Say not, 'Behold an hour of my life is gone,' but rather, 'I have lived an hour.' "

To be perfectly frank about it, this "but business" to which Aunt Selma was addicted for a time, ran in our family. I had a case of it for years. I would catch myself saying, "I should have done this, but . . ." "I was all set to get this good break, but . . ." "I should have gotten that appointment, but . . ." You can certainly develop a but-phobia or a but-neurosis this way. Before you ever get around to some solid, positive thinking on matters, back in your mind, unless you are careful, the wrong "but" may stubbornly be blocking your higher intentions.

"I'd like to do this, but . . ." often plunged me into moods of deep indecision. During my undergraduate years when I took work in drama, I really thought I was a paradigm for acting. There was a fellow named Macdonald Carey and another by name of Walter Fleischmann and a third named Clancy Cooper in my classes and I thought I had considerable more talent than they. I was that good, *but,* I reminded myself, I was not destined to get the breaks. All three of these classmates went on to stardom. I should have made it, I told myself, but . . .

Then, like Aunt Selma, I got to thinking. It seems so simple now. It was so complicated then. All you need do is imagine that B-U-T is a fence and if things continually keep going against you, it may be that you are on the wrong side, the wrong side of B-U-T. The assignment is to get on the other side. This is really not so difficult if you remember that the obvious and easiest escape passage is, of course, through "U."

A TV talent agency in Los Angeles recently advertised for

new sounds, new faces, new shapes and sizes. It insisted that stereotyped forms are out. The unusual is in. The approach in the movie capital is not to find someone who is like someone, as was once the case, but to discover someone who is different. The idea is not, "I'd like to get into the movies, *but* I have a big nose," rather, "They did not think I'd be a screen attraction, *but* I have a big nose!" It is not a case of "I'd like to be an actress, but I'm lean and lanky and six feet tall," rather, "They didn't think I could make it, *but* they needed someone lean and lanky and six feet tall." The other side of BUT can be the other side of "U."

A case in point was Michael Dunn, a man three feet ten inches tall, weighing less than eighty pounds. Perhaps you saw him in *The Ballad of the Sad Cafe* and if you did you laughed and wept and wondered as everyone did at the magic spell he wove. He made us realize that a dwarf can be a giant and that the other side of *but* can make you stand as straight and tall as any man.

Is it possible that the BUT in most of our problems and challenges may be the axis upon which our decisions can most successfully be made to turn? Is it perhaps at this very point that we recognize our greatest strength and learn to master our deepest weakness? Take a specific case in your social relationship. Say there is someone you would really like to trust a bit more or be more friendly with or have as a closer friend, but there is a *but* about him that creates a psychological or esthetic block. He is a fine person, *but* he smokes too much. She is such fun to be with, *but* she talks too much. He is a lovely guy, *but* he takes himself too seriously. Now, how do you get around these "buts" and how do you handle these situations when they have to do not with yourself, *but* with others?

A serendipitous fable may help.

Once upon a time in the ancient country of Ceylon (Serendip) a farmer had a goat. A she-goat. Well-marked, healthy and handsome with a naturally groomed beard and sparkling goatish eyes, it was the pride of the herd. But it butted. It butted its mates and it butted its master and one day it even butted its master's mistress. So the farmer got rid of it. He sold it to a wealthy city man who knew nothing about the habits of goats. All the city man knew was that he had a young son who was sick and that a doctor had told him the best remedy for the boy would be goat's milk, a pint a day.

So the goat, whose name was Amphibalus, was put into a padded box and brought to the estate of the rich man. No sooner was it released in the yard than it butted the servants, butted the gardener and butted Weeree, the sick boy's shaggy dog. When the boy's father indignantly strode into the yard to reason with Amphibalus, she butted him too.

Now the sick youngster, Dugowara by name, who had watched the proceedings from his bed in an upstairs room, clapped his hands and rocked with laughter, laughter which had not been heard in the old mansion since Dugowara was stricken. The father rushed up the stairs and breathlessly asked if his son was all right.

"Of course, I am all right!" Dugowara told him. "I have not seen anything as wonderful and amusing since the players were here on my last birthday! Amphibalus is beautiful!"

"She may be beautiful," the father agreed, rubbing his backside, "but she must go. She is a butter."

"No, no, father!" argued Dugowara. "She is a milk giver!"

"She may be a milk giver, but she is a butter."

"No, father," Dugowara corrected. "She may be a butter, *but* she is a milk giver!"

The emphasis the sick boy put on the words caused the father to stand in deep thought. Then he came quietly to his son's bed, sat down and took the youngster's hands.

"You are right, Dugowara," he said. "Amphibalus is first of all a milk giver. We must always remember that."

He called the servants and the gardener and instructed them that they should treat the goat with special respect and care, even to staying out of its way and of preparing a comfortable stall with plenty of food for Amphibalus at milking time.

When this was done, Dugowara summoned the shaggy dog who came and nuzzled his nose on the bed. Dugowara stroked the dog affectionately. "Weeree," he said, "Amphibalus is very dear to me, as you are. Sometimes you run away, but you are my friend. Sometimes Amphibalus will butt, but she is my remedy."

As the days went by it was almost as if the goat had heard the bedroom conversation and began to appreciate her role in life. Came the day when the rich man and his wife stood in their son's bedroom and looked down into the yard through tears of joy, for there were Dugowara, Weeree and Amphibalus playing together as if they had been friends since time began.

Transposed to the problem of the person who is "fine but he smokes too much," the fable urges us to see the "fine side" and make allowance for the smoke with which we may occasionally be butted. After all, he who insists on perfection in others may be wanting in perfection in himself.

Or, if "she is such fun, but she talks too much," how about taking another look at the qualities she has that make for fun. It may be that an understanding attitude toward her could change her attitude if it needs changing, just as the decision in favor of Amphibalus cured the she-goat's butting.

And if you think that "he is a lovely guy, but takes himself too seriously," how about giving him another glance? Would he be equally lovely if he altered this particular trait? And if it needs altering, isn't there a chance that your ability to see his *best* traits will improve his *lesser* ones? After all, what we call rational grounds for our reactions may be irrational attempts to justify a buttishness within ourselves.

My Aunt Selma used to be that way and so did I. Truth is, I might still be that way had it not been for the Princes of Serendip. Their insistence that our personalities are shaped and fashioned by our points of view helped me to see more clearly and reach around more easily to the other side of *but*.

20

UNTANGLING
OUR TANGLED WEBS

$\mathcal{T}$ he best argument I ever heard
against the use of hallucino-
genic drugs came from a spider.

It came shortly after I had taken peyote for the sake of
research. My friends who had experimented with LSD and
psilocybin which, like peyote, act upon the nervous system
and produce all sorts of mood expansions and distortions,
had urged me to get into the act. This was during the days
when psychedelic trips were definitely the in-thing and
when anyone who wasn't in was obviously a square.

Between LSD, which is lysergic acid diethylamide, and
psilocybin, which is a derivative of the "sacred mushroom,"
and peyote, which is mescaline extracted from the Mexican

cactus, I chose the latter. Lowliest of the psychedelic family, peyote seemed to me more earthy than the others even though it is bitter stuff and nauseating no matter how much orange juice is used to kill the acrid taste.

Why did I take it? As I have said, for research. Mostly because I wanted to be able to better communicate with people who came to me with their visions, impressions, hopes, and concerns induced by the craze, now passing, for hallucinogenic experiences.

Enter the spider.

The spider came via research by several arachnidologists (spider studiers) particularly Dr. Peter Witt of the University of New York in Syracuse. In Dr. Witt's intriguing work he discovered that when spiders receive injections of mescaline they begin to weave highly erratic webs, louse up their silk production, and generally upset their nervous system. Under normal circumstances a spider's web is a work of art, enchantment, and mathematical precision. Here you have a creature the size of a fingertip which produces its own silk, emits it through a thousand hairlike tubes, creates a gossamer mesh out of apparent nothingness, and hangs it in space with such infinite skill it is barely visible to the naked eye.

"If we have a web with twenty radii," Dr. Witt reported to the American Association for the Advancement of Science, "and thirty spiral turns, there are six hundred points where the threads cross each other, to say nothing of the frame and the hub and their additional points to be analyzed."

The fact is that a study of the proportions, convulsions and intricacies of the web-weaving techniques of the average spider became so complex that Dr. Witt enlisted the aid of a computer. This is to say that the brain of the spider, or whatever it is that directs the spinning and weaving of a web, challenged the best brain power modern man has yet devised.

"I believe," said Dr. Witt, "there is no other animal or living being which leaves such a perfect record of its movements as does the spider in the daily orb of weaving its web."

The Cross Spider, whose professional name is *Araneus Diadematus,* builds a web every morning in about twenty minutes and, as far as is known, constructs it at the same hour and under the same conditions as do his fellow *Araneus Diadematuses.* Though the webs look alike, they vary from spider to spider, showing both a likeness and an individuality, to say nothing of their phenomenal perfection and precision. That is, until you give the spiders a shot of mescaline. Then their silk production is affected, their autonomic nervous system is jarred, and an uncertainty and frustration show up in their behavorial patterns.

What has this to do with you and me? Simply this. The nervous system of the Cross Spider is sufficiently comparable to the nervous system of man to present an interesting analogy, enough alike, at least, to add a provocative chapter to our insight into the world of serendipity. For while the Princes of Serendip continually remind us of the profitable benefits of unexpected discoveries, they caution us about the disastrous effects of self-induced stimulation.

Remember the story of the intoxicated sahib? Fez cocked over his ear, he staggered up to the Princes and with a drunken flourish exclaimed, "The greatest treasures, my beloved, are found in the fermented fruit of the vine! If you have any doubts about it, just look at me!"

"We *are* looking at you," the Princes said, "and that is why our doubts increase. *Whatever robs a man in order to rule him, is not fit to be his ruler.*"

Then they went on to tell about the tangled webs we weave when we begin to deceive not others, but ourselves.

Hence the spider.

The spider teaches us lessons in weaving the web of life. He does a good job as long as he obeys his innate nature. But, you say, in the case of the Cross Spider, he could not help it since men experimented on him and outside powers blasted him with a dose of mescaline. Right! That is just the point. Perhaps a spider cannot help it, but usually *we* can. We who boast of being God's highest creation generally have it in our power not to be ruled by that which would rob us of our ability to rule. I am not talking only about hallucinogenics or narcotics or addictive drugs, but about the common lapses when we let down our guard against anger, envy, worry, revenge, or any of the "seven-times-seven-deadly sins." These can literally wreck our web of life.

Incidentally spiders more than any other insects are compared to humans in the mythological flow of history. For one thing, they are found wherever homo sapiens is found, from pole to pole, and in some places which men have not yet conquered. There is, for example, the aquatic spider which builds its nest under water and fills its silken habitat with air as if to demonstrate to oceanographers the possibilities of sub-sea habitation. Certain spiderlings are astronauts, letting the wind balloon them into space while they retain the ability to create their own reentry parachutes by means of their silk-producing glands. If they should lose a leg they can grow another by the process of regeneration. When the female spider is ready to lay her eggs she prepares a silken sheet, deposits her precious treasure of 100 to 300 eggs, and covers them with another sheet of silk, some species dragging the unhatched brood along with them wherever they go.

There are wolf spiders which pursue their prey, particularly male wolf spiders pursuing females, from which we may get our term for the whistling "wolves." There are trapdoor spiders, lying in wait, as do some shopkeepers for impulse-buying customers. There are tunnel spiders who shun the company of others and enjoy the dark. There are jumping spiders which are fidgety and erratic. But most spiders, like most humans, ask for little more than to be left unmolested so that they may weave their webs and raise their young and live their lives in a span that covers no more than a single year. A proverb says, "The spider's touch, how exquisitely fine, feels at each thread and lives along the line."

In American Indian lore we find the legend of the Spider Man whose strands connected earth with heaven, while in Hinduism there are stories of gods who united the essence of darkness with the essence of light by means of webs. Therefore the unseen powers that held the universe together were often thought of as cosmic beings reverently known as spider gods.

Every good Moslem knows how a spider saved the life of their Prophet. When Mohammed fled from Mecca with a price upon his head, he hid in a cave while the pursuing Koreishites were hot on his trail. He would surely have been detected and killed had it not been that a spider, conceivably *Araneus Diadematus,* spun a web across the entrance to the cave. When the captain of the Koreishites saw this he exclaimed, "No need to go in there. See the web. No one has come and gone into that entrance recently."

Or consider the true story of Robert Bruce, fourteenth century King of the Scots. Bruce was attacked by the English, retreated to Ireland, and was presumed to be dead. While hiding on the island of Rathbin, he bemused himself by watching a spider on the ceiling. Six times the spider doggedly tried to fix its anchor strand on a beam so that it could build its web. On the seventh try it succeeded. "This spider has taught me what to do," Bruce vowed. "Six times have *I* failed to regain my throne!" So saying he left Rathbin, gathered a volunteer army, marched to the English garrison in Turnberry Castle, and eventually regained the Scottish throne.

I have a serendipitous nephew, Richard Bach, whose book, *Stranger to the Ground,* was condensed in *Reader's Digest* several years ago. Dick is a flyer and feels more at ease in the air than on the whirling earth. Recently he and several other courageous young daredevils barnstormed the Midwest in what they called *The Great American Flying Circus.*

In true serendipity fashion they had no stated itinerary and their philosophy was that everything is under infinite guidance, all events are meaningful, everything is always in divine order, and life, like airplanes, is structured to fit its environment. There are no orphans in the sky.

Dick flew his antique biplane over a town, the other equally ancient planes joined him and engaged in stunts and dogfights and acrobatic maneuvers until a crowd gathered. Then they landed in a farmer's field, made friends with the citizenry, and took them up for rides in their ancient sky-skiffs at $3 a head.

What has this to do with spiders? Well, on one occasion when they had their map spread out on the ground and were contemplating which route they should follow, a spider crawled over the map. Dick looked at it and said, "Let's follow the spider's route!" So they did with great success! Now obviously there is no place for mescaline in this kind of adventuring, and you had better believe it that there is no such thing as chance! The whole procedure is given a light and lovely touch, for I know of no young man who insists more fully than Richard, an extremely careful flyer, that *"Whatever robs a man in order to rule him, is not fit to be his ruler."*

According to Freud, if the sight of a spider induces neurotic anxiety this is presumed to be an unconscious association of the spider with the phallic mother. But to see beauty in the web releases fear, especially when the web is perfectly spun. But again, if the loops of the web are loose, the meshes erratic, the form confused as if an outer force had gained the upper hand, naturally this could evoke convulsive reactions.

I have a hunch that if the Princes of Serendip were walking the earth today or flying the sky they would be saying, "Untangle your tangled webs! Get control! Do not let drugs or passions or outside powers rule your life or spoil your spinning! Trust your innate power!"

One way to do this is to take the mixed-up threads one by one instead of disassembling the entire web. Take each strand and "live along the line." Examine each situation and see what you can do to straighten it out. Life *is* a web of our own spinning, but we can be master builders. Try honestly and sincerely to see where you have made a faulty loop or taken a wrong turn along the way. See where you can strengthen and improve your anchor strands even if it means a seventh try.

In a recent radio broadcast titled "Men and Molecules," Dr. Charles Reed, psychologist at Temple University, said, "The computer is so equipped that it can actually 'regurgitate' the spider's web, or, in a sense, reconstruct it. We measure the size of the central angles. We get the number of spiral turns and the number of radii. We compute the total length of the thread used by the spider. We compute the areas of all the zones of the web. We ask the computer to do other operations which would be extremely tedious for a human clerk as, for example, find out how many oversized angles are there, or how many angles are there which are larger than the sum of the two adjacent angles. The computer patiently goes around and asks of each central angle, 'Are you larger than your two adjacents?' then measures them to see if they are and tallies them for us. It then takes these dimensions which it has constructed for us so that we can ask, 'Is there a noticeable difference between the webs built before and after the mescaline treatment?' "

I can hear the Princes of Serendip exclaim, "Wonderful! Truly wonderful! Think of that! But, O my scientists, and O my brothers, and O my dear computer, while you are making your tabulations, calculations, suppositions, hypotheses and conclusions, never forget that in the creature Man no less than in *Araneus Diadematus,* a divine life and law are moving which if left to pursue their innate course unhindered will weave a web of life beyond compare! Continue your experiments, to be sure, for the best argument I ever heard against the use of hallucinogenic drugs came from your spiders, but keep the record clear by remembering our saying, *'Whatever robs a man in order to rule him is not fit to be his ruler.'* "

21

I HEARD
A FOREST SINGING

*W*henever I water the philodendron in my California study,
I think of serendipity. For a long time it was merely a
decorative plant conveniently filling a bare spot between
bookshelves and windows, but that was before I met Cleve
Backster.

Mr. Backster, scientist, technician, and polygraph expert
(lie detector), also had a philodendron in his New York
City office and he, too, thoughtfully watered it one day.
When he did so, however, he stumbled headlong into a
startling serendipitous discovery.

This is what happened: as he poured the water into the
root area of the plant, he wondered how long it took for

the moisture to reach the leaves. In the uncounted years of philodendron history (*philo* meaning love, *dendron* tree, according to the Greek), many a housewife or florist or gardener may have wondered about the same thing. Cleve Backster, however, with his scientific twist of mind, decided to measure the time factor with a polygraph, using the psychogalvanic reflex index as his guide. So he deftly attached a pair of PGR electrodes to a leaf of the plant and made the necessary adjustments in the circuitry.

Serendipity was waiting in the wings, so to say, and Backster gradually realized that the PGR tracing was amazingly similar to that registered by human beings in their emotional responses. Thoughtfully he gazed from the graph on the chart to the silent philodendron. What, he wondered, was going on here? This had nothing to do with the water or moisture rising from root to leaf. Did the philodendron have human reflexes? If so, what would be its response if he pinched its leaves, or if he singed one with a match?

At the very moment that he plotted this in his mind, *even before he reached for a match,* the plant recorded an abrupt pattern similar to that of a person instinctively registering anxiety.

Backster's scientifically oriented mind, however, was not inclined to be carried away by the Princes of Serendip. After all, he had a twenty-year status in the field of polygraph research and the government had frequently called him in to testify at Congressional hearings on polygraph technology. He was not one to put his reputation on the line or face the scientific world half-cocked with a serendipitous theory. So he kept his suppositions to himself and there followed months of secret experimentation, not only on plants but on an incredible variety of other single-cell organisms all the way from the lowly amoeba to scrapings "from the roof of the mouth of humans."

Finally, after some three years, he felt inclined to make a preliminary report sufficiently newsworthy and sensational to catch the imagination of the Fourth Estate, to say nothing about the Fifth: radio and television. Soon scientific journals were running guarded headlines: "Do Plants Have Feelings?" "Can Plants Experience Human-Like Emotions?" "Does Nature Have Secret Signals of Joy and Pain?"

Popular periodicals were more outspoken. They said, "Do Your Plants Love You?" "Please Don't Hurt the Daisies!" "You Are Being Watched by Your African Violets!" "Cleve Backster, the Man Who Reads Nature's Secret Signals!"

Now do you see why when I water my ubiquitous philodendron I often pause and gaze in depth at the "tree of love?" After all, one of my earliest heroes was a naturalist named Luther Burbank who insisted that plants respond to love and tender care. I knew a woman who used to walk through her garden talking intimately to the growing things. I researched the Edward Bach remedy people in Surrey, England, who believe that each human personality has its counterpart in the essence of a flower. I visited with a professor in Lucknow, India, who was persuaded that plants play a part in the transmigration scheme. I even had an aunt who claimed she saved one of her precious house plants from a withering death by setting it reverently on the family Bible!

Truth is, I must admit to a secret attachment. Ever since we established our British Columbia retreat, I have felt an affinity for nature never experienced in the whir of city life where most of my days are spent. In my woodland retreat I have often felt the scream of pain emitted by a tree when the screeching power of the chain saw pierced its maze of arteries. I have caught the tremor of the towering pine and tamarack when a fire hungrily devoured a ten-mile stand of timber. I even sensed the shudder of the scrubby trees I grubbed out for our cabin clearing, and many were the times I walked through secret trails at dawn or dusk and heard a forest singing.

Naturally I had been harboring thoughts about Cleve Backster and his research ever since I first read his story, and as his popularity grew I wondered how his serendipitous discovery was affecting his life. Did he have a cosmic awareness about the total overview of what he had found? Could he help but feel that he might be a link between the known and the unknown, between the phenomenal world and the "real," between plant and man and even perhaps between so-called inanimate and animate forces as well? In other words, how can a man stumble through serendipity's doors without remaining for a moment, at least, upon his knees?

Then, not long ago, I flew up into the Laurentian hill country in Quebec province to spend several days at a yoga convention. Here were swamis, ministers, a rabbi, yoga adepts, college students, and representatives of many schools of thought from various parts of the world. And by an auspicious fate, who should appear on this spiritually-scientifically-oriented program but Cleve Backster, polygraph and all, to share his research experimentation with our six hundred delegates.

So we met.

Who was it said, "Give me five minutes with a man and I will have an arc whereby to describe the circumference of his life?" I had several days to catch the Backster arc.

Those who had written about him described him as "quiet, polite, serious, studious, scholarly, a man of integrity with the cautious mind of a scientist," and so on.

I was prepared to concur in all this, but the clearest response I got was that here is a man whose life has suddenly taken an inexplicable turn toward scientific sensitivity, by which I mean a recognition that beyond and within the physical sciences is a subliminal factor which is as much a part of natural law as so-called verifiable facts. Here was a man who, in the words of Dr. Samuel Johnson, "refuses to vilify what he cannot fully comprehend."

Cleve Backster had not always been of this temperament. By his own admission he had been an agnostic, double-daring faith to come to terms with logic, chary of parapsychology, tongue in cheek about metaphysics. Now since his serendipitous experience, since the philodendron and some three years of charting and testing in this field, he seemed to me possessed by a sense of inner wonder, as one who has stood in awe upon a new planet in inner space.

It is always refreshing to find a man captivated by an idea and governed by a cause, ready to face the skepticism and frequent scorn of those who have never broken the sound barrier of the physical universe. It was an inspiration to all of us who heard Cleve Backster and who believed that perceptivity could conceivably be a pool of universal consciousness, to realize that though he had not lost his scientific cool, he had caught hold of the warmth of the onward-going quest.

Most dramatic of all his tests was that involving the death of brine shrimp and their effect upon the response of the philodendron. Backster had devised a sophisticated system whereby a bowlful of shrimp was automatically dumped into boiling water without the presence of anyone in the room, excepting the plant. This was a complex, precision-timed experiment under highly qualified test conditions. At the instant the shrimp were immersed, the recording needle of the polygraph leaped frantically in a movement paralleling agony in a human being. Backster repeated the experiment innumerable times, putting the shrimp device in one room and the plant (*Draena Massangeana*) in another. The result and reaction were the same as before. Then he put up barriers in the form of insulation, lead-lined containers, and even a Faraday cage, in attempts to "jam the communication." (The cage consists of a grounded metallic screen to insure a space free from electrostatic fields.) Again, the same response. Nothing apparently could prevent the plant from "feeling" the distresses of its fellow creatures. To all intents and purposes an invisible chain linked cell to cell and neither distance nor enclosures imposed noticeable limitations.

Backster said to me, "The whole thing shook me up. It shook my life and my belief or disbelief about things. It really did."

It shook me up, too, but in a most wonderful way, for I have always had a hunch that truth is truth wherever found, and that there is also a hidden truth which the polygraph in the probing hands of an inquisitive scientist may be beginning to perceive. If, according to phylogenetic law, we humans *have* passed through all former biological stages before our birth as humans on Planet Earth, is it not possible that we may respond to the impulses and signals of all that responds to us? Can we perhaps actually *feel* the pain of a plant or *hear* the scream of a tree or *sense* the hurt—or aspiration—of unicellular existence in its upward climb in the same way that it responds to us?

However it may be, something has always told me that this old world of ours is tied together with the strings of God more tightly than we know.

And as for serendipity, since it has already been involved in man's outward reach into space, why shouldn't it lead us inwardly into the secrets of a subtle leaf alive with life?

22
THE ULTIMATE SERENDIPITY

*T*he story of everyman is this: If he leaves his father's house and walks a fairly straight line, every step he takes brings him nearer home. He may think he is going away, but he is actually coming back. This is strict ecology, karma, the mystery of life, causal law, pure math. This is the ultimate serendipity and as it happened to the Princes of Serendip, so it is bound to happen to you and me.

Came the day when our three royal vagabonds awoke one spring morning to see the sunrise over their father's kingdom. Their odyssey, to all intents and purposes, was ending where it began. They stood on the knoll of

159

Kennwata viewing old scenes, domes of temples, sheep in the fields, the neatly thatched homes of the king's subjects, the open gates of the castle on the hill. Nothing had changed yet everything was different.

"The true eye of life is the mind," said the youngest Prince.

"Every moment of travel is a coming home," mused the second.

"I can hear our father greeting us with his 'Good Morning,' " commented the eldest, "as if we had never been away."

They paid their homage to the rising sun and started walking toward their father's home single file.

It was my fault. I got Richard Strauss mixed up with Johann Strauss. The first had a heavy-handed Wagnerian touch in his solid and scholarly works, while the second was the renowned waltz king who gave us such feathery pieces as *Blue Danube, Wine, Women and Song,* and *Die Fledermaus.*

Admittedly I know little about these things, but here we were in Vienna, city of operatic lore, and my wife said there was no excuse for not attending the opera even though we had just arrived in town and curtain time was one short hour away. So I telephoned the hotel desk, was told there was an opera by Strauss and off we went, only to realize when we were handed our programs that we were in for *Ariadne* by Richard Strauss.

I have come to live by principles of serendipity, but this seemed a bit too much. Weary from our drive-it-yourself trip from Trieste, bugged by a bad hotel situation, breaking our necks in typical American style to get to the theatre on time, and now stashed into a cramped loge with two other couples, I was sharply tested in my serendipitous conviction.

The overture began, the curtain went up on a weighty and ominous scene of rocks and rolling surf, and it occurred to me that if one is not careful and gets overly tired, life can be nothing but a series of rising curtains and overtures in a minor key. *Ariadne* was the last thing I needed on this sultry summer night. I could have done very well without the scene I was seeing: Ariadne, bemoaning the agonizing futility of unrequited love, is on a deserted, rockbound island waiting death.

Now there is a plot to sing about for two hours and twenty minutes including intermission. I was ready to head back to the hotel during the entr'acte, but this was Vienna, my wife is a romanticist and sufficiently frugal not to get her thirty dollars money's worth even if it kills both the tragedienne and us. So we stayed. We stayed while Richard Strauss figured out how he could break our hearts with oboe and bassoon and shatter our resistance with kettle drum and cymbal, persuading us against our will to identify with tear-stained Ariadne. No use. We all have to go sometime, Ariadne, and the sooner you get it over with the sooner we can get some air, catch a cool drink, and go to bed.

There are times when all of us are caught in seemingly unserendipitous situations, when for the life of us we cannot figure out why we are where we are or what brought us here. At such moments, instead of weeping, I begin to wonder, and rather than resisting I reflect on how often some later period makes the present meaningful. When I am lowest in faith I am often highest with God.

And there was Ariadne languishing for a lover who never came and praying for her death too long in coming. Johann Strauss, I was sure, would have gotten us out of this situation in three-quarter time, but not Richard. With mournful strains and melancholy measures that addled the brain, Ariadne groaned her way to ever deepening despair.

But suddenly I was roused by a striking stage effect and an arresting change of pace. A ship, real as any that sailed the seas, came gliding across the theatrical waves straight out of the pathway of the rising sun. I could almost feel the spray. I could touch the wind. The sagging form and heaving bosom of Ariadne told us this is Death.

Fair enough. It would soon be finis.

Then the master stroke, the sudden denouement, the chord triumphant! The agile, athletic meistersinger who stepped from the ship with burst of song and leaped to the pinnacle of rock, who caught a halo from the sun's ecstatic rays, was not Death but Life. He was, in fact, Ariadne's lover come to wipe the tears from her eyes and lift the years of sorrow from her heart.

Serendipity? Eventually the ultimate: Death is Life and Lover, and those who know this mystery also know that life's opera must by all odds have a Richard as well as a Johann touch.

The Princes passed the home of the woodsman Sanda-wani. This wiry, smiling workman was planting seedlings on the valley slope and from the order and arrangement of his work, he might have been setting out rows of fruit trees in the king's orchard.

"This is what you were doing when we left our father's kingdom years ago," said the Princes.

"Years ago?" echoed Sandawani and looked at them as if he did not understand. Quickly he caught himself and said, "You have traveled far?"

"Of course we have traveled far," said the youngest Prince somewhat annoyed.

"And I," said Sandawani, hardly pausing in his work, "have been nowhere. I have felled trees for both fuel and

*building, and have planted always a few more than I cut
down. You have traveled. I have not, yet we are all
together in this moment of time."*

*He poured water gently on a seedling and with warm
hands pressed the moist earth around its tender roots.*

*"Strange," said the Princes, "in foreign lands we were the
ones who imparted wisdom, but here in our father's
kingdom wisdom speaks even from a woodsman who, it
seems, used to listen to us."*

Picking up strangers is a matter we must decide on the
level of our consciousness by whatever standard of judgment seems right. I have my own intuitive method and it is
strictly mine. At any rate, something told me to stop and
pick up this young man. I was going his way, envious of his
shock of golden hair, interested in the ankh medallion over
his blue open-necked shirt, but most of all I was mindful of
the time when I, being of college age, was also forced to
hitch a ride.

In twenty miles I had his story. A farmer's son, from
Ohio, a year at Oberlin, a drop out, a hippie year, a futile
quest for meaning, a year of disillusionment, a few trips on
LSD, Uncle Sam, Vietnam. A war casualty, recurrent
physical disability, home, a year at school, Easter now, and
on his way to see his girl in Phoenix, a hundred miles
away.

Most of our talk was about war and wars and body
counts and whether massacres are for real, and every once
in a while something brought us around to the Sermon on
the Mount.

"I used to like to hunt," he said. "I could look a deer
straight in the eye down the gun barrel and pull the trigger,
for the fun of it. Squirrels and rabbits, too. One minute
they were alive. The next minute they were dead. I was God."

Boot camp. More God. Training for God against non-God. From the art of self-defense to self-preservation. From killing the seen to killing the unseen. He had been proud of his prowess. Now he sat in silence watching the road unfold as he thought whatever he was thinking.

Beside me sat myself. Beside me, conscience. Beside me sat a listener who once sat listening to the Sermon on the Mount.

My companion was unclear as to when the change in his thinking took place. He thought it had already started before he was wounded. It intensified during his recovery. It deepened when he met the girl he was going to see. She was a nurse, a pacifist. He disagreed with her on one strategic point. She was of the opinion that war was already obsolete in the mind of man. He didn't. He felt we still had something to discover. The goal of war is peace, he thought, but mankind has not yet seen enough of it, has not really felt the horror and shock of it. To mankind generally it is still not quite real. Normandy, Berlin, Nagasaki, Hiroshima, Vietnam and so on, not enough. Not yet real to those who never felt the fighting except on TV.

The ultimate? He didn't know. He only knew that somewhere, at some point in the search for victory someone had to stumble on the greatest victory, peace through love.

The Princes of Serendip paused at a chapel close to the palace. The youngest Prince said, "You would think the bells would ring for us now that we are coming home."

The eldest said, "I hear them loud and clear."

Their brother Prince stood listening and agreed.

"Yesterday," said the chapel keeper, "before you went away, I lit three candles and three incense sticks."

He was a young man and you would have thought he

knew better than to say, "Yesterday," when everyone knew it was years and years ago that the sons of the king went away. But that was what the chapel keeper said and the Princes let it go at that because the young man had by no means changed since their departure. And when they entered the chapel there were the three candles scarcely burned and there were the incense sticks as if they had just been lighted.

The Princes approached the altar and knelt down. Each intoned a prayer and then the youngest said, "It was not yesterday we left. It was now."

The second said, "The people we met along the way are with us here and their candles burn as slowly and patiently as our own."

Out of the silence the words of the eldest Prince came softly and full of quiet joy. "Thank you for laughter," he said, without so much as mentioning why he said it.

And the bells began to ring.

The other night a friend of mine insisted it was time I saw a blue movie. "My God," he said, "all you do is work and write [as though writing were not work] and you don't know what's happening in the world."

So we went to a blue movie, an X, double X, triple X picture or however they classify them, and though we were early there was a crowd of made-to-order shills a block long impatient to put their three dollars on the line and get inside.

My friend was right when he said I did not know much about this world which has crawled up through the nets of the League for Decency and the PTA and the boards of censorship and all the other guardians of virtue, and emerged more nude and nasty than any burlesque against which my preacher uncle used to fulminate. At least I thought so. However, according to my friend, the nastiness is only in the eye of the beholder and if you have the right perspective, nude bodies in naked action are unadulterated art all the way from what the preachers used to call sin to what the Bible talked about as sodomy.

It was a movie designed to blow your brain and I wondered where unadulterated art could go from here. My friend said we could rest assured that someone would dream up even more and brighter forms of saturnalia. One thing was sure, the defenders of decency were as dead at this moment as the WCTU and as impotent as evangelists who used to detonate against free love.

I heard of a girl who said, "I had to see for myself what these films are like. I wore dark glasses. (Yellow.) Maybe I'm a square but I left before it was over with a feeling of shame and anger at America."

Take heart! Always there is the outside chance that on this strange unfolding serendipitous road, where ultimate Death is Life, and where the tender roots of Peace lie slumbering in the soil of War, blue movies with their sodomy and sex may prove to hold a new respect for the esthetic and moral life of man. You never know about these things, especially if you have walked with the Princes from the ancient land of Serendip, and back again.

So they entered their father's house, and the king was on his way to a cabinet meeting in the throne room. When he glanced their way and saw them he paused and raised a hand in greeting.

"Good morning," he said, as if they had never been away.

"Father," said the youngest Prince, "I think you should know why we went away. You see, we knew it would be difficult for you to decide which one of us should rule the

kingdom after you are gone. So we thought we would make it easy for you. Ordinarily the eldest is the rightful successor, but since we knew you loved us all equally, we intended simply to go out of your life. But somehow here we are."

"There is more to it than that," added the second Prince. "We thought that somewhere along our journey we would find the final answer. But we didn't. The final answer was our goal, Father, and since we failed to find it, I am wondering now whether you have any idea how and where it can be found?"

"We did find some lesser goals," the eldest Prince admitted, "at least I did. By a strange discovery it occurred to me that you will never be appointing any of us as your successor because since you always were, you always will be. Nor did we ever actually leave the kingdom, because your kingdom is everywhere. And, finally, how can we take your place since without us you would not be?"

With this the Princes looked at one another as if in a moment of understanding, and when they turned to look at their father he was not there. But in the throne room there were sounds like voices, and a light, brighter than the light of morning streamed through the open doors and covered them.

When I learned of all this through the kindness of the Princes of Serendip, I, too, expected to hear music or chimes or at least the tinkling of a camel's bell. I thought by rights there should be a candle's light or the scent of incense, to say nothing about a vision.

All was strangely, deeply silent. Beautifully silent. It was like a dawning over the world. And quiet laughter.

Just then I felt that all was well.